Push to Open

A Teacher's QuickGuide to Universal Design for Teaching Students on the Autism Spectrum in the General Education Classroom

Lisa Combs

PUBLISHING

P.O. Box 23173
Shawnee Mission, Kansas 66283-0173
www.aapcpublishing.net

PUBLISHING

©2015 AAPC Publishing
P.O. Box 23173
Shawnee Mission, Kansas 66283-0173
www.aapcpublishing.net

Publisher's Cataloging-in-Publication

Combs, Lisa.

  Push to open : a teacher's quick guide to universal design for teaching students on the autism spectrum in the general education classroom / Lisa Combs. -- Shawnee Mission, Kansas : AAPC Publishing, [2014]

    pages ; cm.

    ISBN: 978-1-942197-00-3
    LCCN: 2014952510
    Includes bibliographical references.
    Summary: A series of strategies to make it easier for general education teachers to help students with autism spectrum disorders gain access to and be successful in the general education curriculum. The universal design for learning approach is based on the philosphy that what benefits students with ASD generally also benefits students without disabilities.--Publisher.

    1. Teachers of children with disabilities--Handbooks, manuals, etc. 2. Teaching--Aids and devices. 3. Children with autism spectrum disorders--Education. 4. Autistic children-- Education. 5. Asperger's syndrome--Patients--Education. I. Title.

LC4717 .C66 2014
371.94--dc23   1411

Black and white art: ©www.shutterstock.com

This book is designed in Cambria and Helvetica Neue.

Printed in the United States of America.

Acknowledgments

Over my 27-year career in special education, there are so many people I would like to acknowledge, who have helped to inform the ideas in this book.

First, I would like to acknowledge the hundreds of students with autism and their educational teams who have helped me learn what I regard as the true meaning of "evidence-based practice": the use of expert professional judgment to apply the best research-supported practices, tailored to the individual characteristics of each unique child.

I would also like to acknowledge my work partners: Susan Aebker, DHS, OTR/L, for her amazing expertise in sensory modulation theory and interventions, and Carol Dittoe, MA, CCC/SLP, for how much she has taught me about the intricacies of functional communication. In addition, I would like to thank Heather Bridgman, for exposing me to many of the transformational concepts behind universal design for learning.

I would like to thank Don Sheer, Jan Balbach, and Frank DePalma, without whose vision I would not have had the opportunity over the past four years to put research into practice with hundreds of students and thousands of educators, service providers, and parents through the Miami Valley Autism Coaching Team program.

I would like to thank my husband, retired school administrator Wayne Combs, for his always-wise perspective and "big picture" thinking and for his advice in communicating my message.

I would like to thank my editor, Kirsten McBride, for lending me her patience, wisdom, and experience throughout the writing process, to ensure that my book was all that it could be.

And last, but far from least, I would like to thank elementary teacher Gretchen Rorher, special education paraprofessional Therese Garison, and parent Diana McClain for inspiring me to write this book, with their daily demonstration of how, with teamwork, dedication, and creativity, recommendations made specifically to support a child with autism can be translated in universal ways that end up helping every child in the classroom access a richer educational experience.

Table of Contents

CHAPTER ONE

Automatic Door Openers for Autism: An Overview of the Push to Open Model

We have all encountered situations where we approach a building that we need to enter, but our arms are full of bags, we are on crutches or have a baby in a stroller. There we are – a few inches from gaining access to the location, the services, the goods we need – but we are unable to juggle everything in order to open the door. That is when we are so grateful to see a familiar button within reach ...

This same concept applies to learners on the autism spectrum as they attempt to gain access to the general education environment and curriculum. Students with autism spectrum disorders (ASD) have unique learning profiles, but they have in common some challenges as they strive to learn and progress toward attaining the content standards, social skills, and communication requirements of everyday school life.

While the teacher may not be able to completely "unload" those characteristics, teachers can design their classroom arrangement and climate as well as instructional program in such a way that they remove many of the barriers posed by the school environment, thereby effectively "opening the door" for the student's learning. The beauty of this is that many of the strategies that can open doors to learning for students with ASD are also "best practice" strategies for maximizing learning for ALL students, much in the same way that the "Push to Open" button was designed to assist people with physical disabilities but benefits us all at some point in our lives.

The principle just described is a very rudimentary description of the concept called "universal design for learning" and is the basis of *Push to Open: A Teacher's QuickGuide to Universal Design for Teaching Students on the Autism Spectrum in the General Education Classroom.*

This book does not purport to be an exhaustive analysis of ASD, nor of universal design. Instead, with this book, you will learn more about some of the most common underlying characteristics of autism and how various elements of the environment and instructional methodology can have either a positive or a negative impact on a student's ability to access the opportunities within the general education environment. The focus of *Push to Open* is not on specific individual interventions that may be necessary to supplement services to a student with ASD but on how the general education teacher can proactively design the overall classroom environment and daily instruction to remove barriers for students with ASD while also offering rich and accessible instruction for the rest of the class.

As the incidence of ASD has grown, the learning curve in teaching methodology has been intimidating, to say the least, even for people who have advanced degrees in the instruction of students with disabilities. I have a bachelor's degree and a master's degree in special education for kindergarten through 12th grade and across all disability categories. However, when I took my college courses in the mid-1980s, the incidence of autism was 1 in 10,000. I remember the day my professor covered autism in class. He pointed out the paragraph devoted to it in our textbook, showed us a 20-minute filmstrip of a nonverbal child with classic autism being instructed using discrete trial training, and said, "Don't worry about committing much of this to memory. The likelihood of you ever teaching a child with autism is slim to none."

Fast forward in time 27 years, and now the most recent statistics reveal that the prevalence of ASD is as high as 1 in 68 ("CDC Estimates," 2014). As a result, most, if not all, intervention specialists have served a student on the autism spectrum by now, and a growing number of general education teachers have some experience with ASD as well. According to the U.S. Department of Education's National Center for Education Statistics, students with autism are served in a variety of educational placements, ranging from full-time general education classes to full-time placement in separate classrooms (Snyder & Dillow, 2013). However, as the educational community has strived to fully implement the Individuals with Disabilities Education Improvement Act (IDEIA), and we have gained a better understanding of the true spectrum of skills and abilities that comprises autism and its related disorders, we have grown in our understanding that many students on the spectrum, if not most, are best served in the general education environment for at least a portion of their educational day.

A gap has developed between the increasing number of students with ASD being served in the general education classroom and the number of teachers who have received formal training in methodologies for teaching students with ASD. Thus, according to the National Research Council, personnel preparation "remains one of the weakest elements of effective programming for children with autistic spectrum disorder" (2001, p. 225). Adding substantially to this challenge is the extraordinarily heterogeneous nature of the disability. Current research has identified evidence-based practices but also confirmed that there is no one ideal program or no single instructional approach that works for all students with ASD because each child has a unique profile of characteristics and learns best in a number of different contexts (Aspy & Grossman, 2008).

While most general education teachers are strongly committed to the pursuit and application of research-based strategies for literacy, mathematics, and other content areas, it is difficult for any teacher to work through the amount of information available on strategies for instructing students on the autism spectrum, much less try to determine which methodologies match the needs of an individual student.

To date, the following methodologies have been identified as meeting the criteria for being considered an "evidence-based practice" according to the National Professional Development Center (NPDC) on Autism Spectrum Disorders (http://autismp-dc.fpg.unc.edu).

Evidence-Based Practices
for Children and Youth With ASD

- Antecedent-Based Interventions (ABI)
- Cognitive Behavioral Intervention
- Differential Reinforcement
- Discrete Trial Training
- Exercise
- Extinction
- Functional Behavior Assessment
- Functional Communication Training
- Modeling
- Naturalistic Intervention
- Parent-Implemented Intervention
- Peer-Mediated Instruction and Intervention
- Picture Exchange Communication System (PECS)
- Pivotal Response Training
- Prompting
- Reinforcement
- Response Interruption/Redirection
- Scripting
- Self-Management
- Social Narratives
- Social Skills Groups
- Structured Play Groups
- Task Analysis
- Technology Aided Instruction
- Time Delay
- Video Modeling
- Visual Supports

(Evidence-Based Practices Briefs, 2014)

A great deal of valuable and useful professional guidance and information is available through the NPDC and other sites devoted to the dissemination of valid, reliable information on evidence-based practices for students with ASD. However, the sheer volume and technical nature of the information can be intimidating to even a seasoned intervention specialist trying to get up to speed, let alone a general educator who is educating a student on the autism spectrum for the first time.

Push to Open provides the general educator a universal design for learning (UDL) approach to creating an educational environment that incorporates many of the evidence-based strategies for learners on the autism spectrum *translated* in a manner that creates simple-to-implement practices for educating ALL learners.

The term "universal design" was originally used by architect Ronald Mace in the 1980s to describe the process of designing environments, products, and services in a manner that would make them of the greatest use and benefit to all people, regardless of their age, ability or health status. (Hall, Meyer, & Rose, 2012). The term was extended in interpretation when the Center for Applied Special Technology (CAST) was formed by a group of education researchers with the mission of exploring how educational outcomes could be improved by the flexible use of educational methods and instructional materials. They, in turn, coined the term "universal design for learning," or UDL ("CAST Through the Years," 2014).

Overview of the Book

Sometimes, complex problems can be resolved with a simple, straightforward solution that benefits everyone. Consider the following example.

As a kindergartener, Tyler had a hard time dealing with the chaos of the beginning of the school day. After a long bus ride and a walk through crowded halls, his day would often begin with a meltdown before he got into the classroom, much less into his seat. The teacher, Mrs. Reardon, thought a visual checklist with pictures might help him understand the morning routine of arriving at kindergarten, because she knew that visual supports are an evidence-based practice for students with ASD. She also knew that interacting with technology was a huge motivator for Tyler.

So now each morning when the students come in from the bus, Mrs. Reardon has already posted the morning routine, with pictures, on the class interactive Smartboard. She is finding that all of the students move more quietly and quickly now that they have a visual checklist to follow. Tyler comes in last – after everyone else is quietly seated – and it is his job to go up and check each item off the list as he completes them. The students even mention when Tyler is absent, "Who is going to cross off our checklist???" Mrs. Reardon reports with a smile, "It turns out Tyler was not the only 5-year-old who could benefit from a visual reminder of the morning routine."

Push to Open: A Teacher's QuickGuide to Universal Design for Teaching Students on the Autism Spectrum in the General Education Classroom provides the general education teacher or support personnel easy-to-implement strategies that will not only remove barriers to learning for students with ASD but will also enhance learning for the majority of students in any classroom, as UDL is intended to do (Hall et al., 2012). The book begins by reviewing the defining characteristics of ASDs and how they may impact the student's access to and participation in the general education environment. Next, we will review the defining characteristics of UDL and explore simple strategies that are of great benefit to the majority of learners. The final aim of the book is to combine that information as a way to help the general education teacher plan and implement targeted strategies to remove specific barriers that are common for learners with ASD through the use of the PTO Planning Form and the PTO QuickTip Sheets (see Appendix).

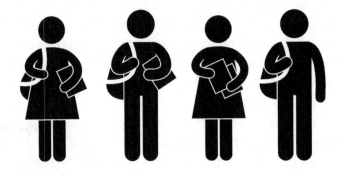

CHAPTER TWO

Principles of Universal Design for Learning

Like any new concept, the principles of universal design for learning can seem overwhelming at first. But, just like Sergeant Joe Friday used to say on the TV show *Dragnet*, this chapter will give you "just the facts"... all that you need to know, and only what you need to know, to get started in the art of universal design as it relates to your students on the autism spectrum.

The Center for Applied Special Technology (CAST) defines universal design for learning (UDL) as follows:

> UDL is a set of principles for curriculum development that give all individuals equal opportunities to learn. UDL provides a blueprint for creating instructional goals, methods, materials, and assessments that work for everyone – not a single, one-size-fits-all solution but rather flexible approaches that can be customized and adjusted for individual needs. ("What Is Universal Design for Learning?," n.d.)

The basic idea behind UDL is that students are unique and bring individual characteristics to the classroom, which then influence how they learn best, based on their strengths, needs, and interests. If you have ever been trained in "differentiation of instruction," these ideas sound familiar to you. For example, you may be familiar with Carol Ann Tomlinson's pioneering developments in how to differentiate content, instructional process, and student products to meet a variety of readiness levels, learning styles, and interests (Tomlinson, 1999). If you are, then you are already "dipping your toes" into the pool of universal design for learning.

Similar to differentiated instruction, UDL concerns itself with how to present instruction in a way that makes new information available to the greatest number of students in the most effective manner. As such, UDL bases its concepts of instruction on three distinct brain networks that impact learning: the Recognition network, the Strategic network, and the Affective network.

These three networks, in turn, may be summed up as the "what," "how," and "why" of teaching and learning (Hall et al., 2012). The "what" part of instruction is how we present information to accommodate different learning styles and learner characteristics. The "how" part is concerned with how the student is going to interact with the content and express what they know. Finally, the "why" aspect focuses on increasing and maintaining student motivation and engagement. CAST (2011) frames these principles succinctly as follows.

WHAT	HOW	WHY
I. Provide Multiple Means of Representation	II. Provide Multiple Means of Action and Expression	III. Provide Multiple Means of Engagement
Perception	Physical action	Recruiting interest
Language, expressions, and symbols	Expression and communication	Sustaining effort and persistence
Comprehension	Executive function	Self-regulation

CAST. (2011). *Universal Design for Learning Guidelines, version 2.0*. Wakefield, MA: Author. Used with permission.

While these are important concepts for us to understand to effectively teach **all** learners, students on the autism spectrum may bring some unique characteristics into your classroom that seem different or present new challenges. This book will help you tweak the "what, how, and why" of your classroom design, behavior management, and daily instruction to better support learners on the autism spectrum.

The Three Brain Networks

The "What"

First, let's look at "what" we teach. In this age of high-stakes testing and accountability, it is generally acknowledged that we must have high expectations for all students and expose every student to opportunities to access and make progress in the general curriculum. It is also widely acknowledged that due to differences in things like preferred learning modalities, processing speed, style, and cognitive differences, not all students learn at the same rate or through the same style of presentation. This is often summed up in the following quote by early American education pioneer George Evans: "All students can learn, though not in the same way on the same day."

You are likely familiar and comfortable with the idea that the best instruction takes into account that some students learn best through auditory channels, some learn best with visual representations, while still others need to have their hands on and interact with materials in order to learn new content. In fact, most of us learn best when we have the opportunity to learn in a variety of activities so that we can hear, see, and interact with the new content being presented to us, often referred to as teaching to individual student learning styles (Tomlinson, 1999; Winebrenner, 1992, 1996). But while this may not be new information to you, there may be characteristics of learners on the autism spectrum that will require special attention to how you present new content. The good news is that the time and energy you devote to tweaking what you are already doing will likely result in better outcomes for many of your students!

The "How"

Just as different students respond differently to presentations of the same content, learners also differ in how they can best express what they know to you as the teacher. Many individual characteristics can impact how students express their knowledge. Language differences, motor differences, and social/behavioral differences are just a few of the characteristics that can particularly impact how students express their knowledge.

We have all had the experience of working with a student who has a great deal of knowledge but has difficulty "getting it out," whether due to expressive language difficulties, written language deficits, or simply the social demands of participating in group discussion. Once again, this book will introduce you to some of the unique characteristics of autism and some instructional strategies that can improve students' effectiveness in communicating what they know.

The "Why"

Finally, but certainly not the least important aspect to consider, is the "why" of teaching and learning. Our individual talents and interests influence how motivated we are to engage in learning activities (Tomlinson, 1999; Winebrenner, 1992, 1996). Many things can impact student motivation and engagement. If you

think back to your own high school days, you probably remember at least one class where you regularly thought to yourself, "WHY do I have to learn this?" Whatever that class was – algebra, English composition, or chemistry – it probably was not your favorite class because you didn't see the importance of it, or how you were going to use what you learned there. However, that class was someone else's very favorite class! *Seeing a purpose in what we are learning and how it applies to our lives* can impact our motivation.

The type of interaction involved in a learning activity can also impact our engagement. Many of us can relate to a time when we attended a professional development workshop and tuned out because the session was all lecture and we needed more interaction. On the other hand, others of us may remember workshops that involved lots of group work and social interactions that made us so uncomfortable that we felt anxious the whole time and just couldn't wait for it to be over! "Cooperative learning" activities may include task demands that are more challenging for shy or introverted folks than they would be for a "social butterfly" who enjoys conversing with others, sharing materials, and working together.

Another factor that can impact our motivation and engagement in learning a new skill is our *level of confidence* (Lavoie, 2007). If you have ever tried something new and outside of your comfort zone, you recognize that your willingness to continue engaging in it is often affected by the degree of success you have as you are learning. For instance, a few years ago, I decided to start playing the guitar. It had been a goal of mine for many years, but each time I attempted it, I tried to learn and memorize each of the basic chords first. I was getting frustrated and I gave up many times.

One day, my son, who plays guitar, suggested that I quit the "drill and kill" of basic chords and instead learn a simple song that I really liked and that only required two or three easy chords. He helped me find a song that fit the bill and suggested I practice it for several days until I could play and sing it perfectly. I did that and suddenly I felt like a rock star! I was highly motivated to learn another song, this time one with three chords! Now, just two years later, I know dozens of chords and hundreds of songs, but more important, I am no longer afraid to learn new ones. I now feel like a competent learner. This is our goal for all of our students – to develop perseverance and resilience in learning new and challenging content in a variety of contexts.

In the following chapters, we will learn which features of ASD may impact the "what," "how," and "why" of learning, along with simple strategies to use in supporting learners with those characteristics in the general education classroom.

CHAPTER THREE

Common Characteristics of Students on the Autism Spectrum

The purpose of the UDL approach to instruction is to proactively plan for a variety of learning styles, strengths, and needs. While it is true that all students come with unique learning profiles, the fact is that learners on the autism spectrum bring some frequently occurring characteristics to the classroom that merit special consideration.

Autism spectrum disorders are characterized by defining characteristics, as well as several other "associated" characteristics (Aspy & Grossman, 2008). We will begin by reviewing the defining characteristics of ASD.

According to the *Diagnostic and Statistical Manual of Mental Disorders, Fifth Edition* (American Psychiatric Association, 2013, p. 50): Autism Spectrum Disorder encompasses two major categories of characteristics:

A. Persistent deficits in social communication and social interaction across multiple contexts

B. Restricted, repetitive patterns of behavior, interests, or activities

The table below gives examples of how these characteristics may be manifested by individuals with ASD.

Diagnostic Criteria Category	Examples of Specific Characteristics That May Be Present
Persistent deficits in social communication and social interaction across multiple contexts, as manifested by the following, currently or by history.	• Deficits in social-emotional reciprocity, ranging, for example, from abnormal social approach and failure of normal back and forth conversation; to reduced sharing of interests, emotions or affect; to failure to initiate or respond to social interactions. • Deficits in nonverbal communicative behaviors used for social interaction, ranging, for example, from poorly integrated verbal and nonverbal communication; to abnormalities in eye contact and body language or deficits in understanding and use of gestures; to a total lack of facial expressions and nonverbal communication. • Deficits in developing, maintaining and understanding relationships, ranging, for example, from difficulties adjusting behaviors to suit various social contexts; to difficulties in sharing imaginative play or in making friends; to absence of interest in peers.
Restricted, repetitive patterns of behavior, interests, or activities, as manifested by at least two of the following, currently or by history.	• Stereotyped or repetitive motor movements, use of objects, or speech (e.g., simple motor stereotypes, lining up toys or flipping objects, echolalia, idiosyncratic phrases). • Insistence on sameness, inflexible adherence to routines, or ritualized patterns or verbal and nonverbal behavior (e.g., extreme distress at small changes, difficulties with transitions, rigid thinking patterns, greeting rituals, need to take the same route or eat the same food every day). • Highly restricted, fixated interests that are abnormal in intensity or focus (e.g., strong attachment to or preoccupation with unusual objects, excessively circumscribed or perseverative interest). • Hyper- or hypo-reactivity to sensory input or unusual interests in sensory aspects of the environment (e.g. apparent indifference to pain/temperature, adverse responses to specific sounds or textures, excessive smelling or touching of objects, visual fascination with lights or movement.

(American Psychiatric Association, 2013, p. 50)

In addition to these criteria, the following conditions must be present:

- Symptoms must be present in the early developmental period (but may not become fully manifest until social demands exceed limited capacities, or may be masked by learned strategies in later life).

- Symptoms cause clinically significant impairment in social, occupational, or other important areas of current functioning.

- These disturbances are not better explained by intellectual disability (intellectual developmental disorder) or global developmental delay. Intellectual disability and autism spectrum disorder frequently co-occur; to make co-morbid diagnoses of autism spectrum disorder and intellectual disability, social communication should be below that expected for general developmental level. (American Psychiatric Association, 2013, pp. 50-51)

It is important to note the word "spectrum" in the name of the diagnosis as a reminder of the variability of the disorder. Thus, as we proceed through this book, keep in mind that when any characteristic or example of a particular student or situation is presented, it represents only one example of how autism can manifest itself. There are myriad ways in which the characteristics of ASD can appear in any particular individual, both in the number of different specific behaviors and in their severity.

The following table shows the DSM-V's delineation of the severity levels of ASD and their associated characteristics:

Severity Level	Social Communication	Restricted, Repetitive Behaviors
Level 3: Requiring very substantial support.	Severe deficits in both verbal and nonverbal communication skills.	Inflexibility of behavior that markedly interferes with functioning.
	Limited initiation of communication with others.	Extreme difficulty coping with change that markedly interferes with functioning.
	Limited response to the communication from others.	Repetitive behaviors or restricted interests that markedly interferes with functioning.
		Great distress when faced with changing focus or action.
Level 2: Requiring Substantial support.	Marked deficits in verbal and nonverbal communication skills.	Inflexible behavior.
	Social impairments evident even when provided supports.	Difficulty coping with change.
	Limited initiation of communication with others.	Restricted interests or repetitive behaviors are evident to a casual observer.
	Limited or inappropriate responses to communication from others.	Distress when faced with changing focus or action.
Level 1: Requiring Support	Noticeable impairments in social communication if supports are not in place.	Inflexibility of behavior causes difficulty in some contexts.
	Difficulty initiating social communications with others.	Difficulty switching between activities.
	Some atypical or unexpected responses to communications from others.	Difficulties with organization that may hamper independence.
	May appear to have decreased interest in social interactions.	

(American Psychiatric Association, 2013, p. 52)

While the diagnostic criteria listed in the DSM-V are a good start-ing point for understanding the needs of students with ASD in the general education classroom, it is helpful to look in greater depth, with examples of how some of the core characteristics of autism can appear in everyday situations. Next, we will take a more in-depth look at some of the core characteristics of ASD that may impact a student's participation in the classroom.

Communication Differences

The following characteristics can greatly impact both receptive (the "what" we teach) and expressive communication (the "how" the student expresses knowledge), as well as the motivation of the learner (the "why" factor of keeping students engaged in the learning process). Given the variability within and among learn-ers with ASD, it is critical to understand the impact of these char-acteristics so that we do not underestimate a student's potential, which might otherwise be camouflaged by deficits in communica-tion. Thus, a key element in effective outcomes for students with autism is the teacher's belief that all students are capable of learn-ing and a determination on the teacher's part to help every stu-dent meet his or her potential (Kluth & Chandler-Olcott, 2008). So, while we must understand the specific deficits that a child with autism may demonstrate, we must always understand it in the context of how we can help remove barriers to learning, rath-er than seeing it as a limitation in what the student can achieve.

Joint Attention

An area of weakness that results in many communication defi-cits for students with ASD involves joint attention, defined as "the ability to coordinate attention and share focus on an event or ob-ject" (Aspy & Grossman, 2008, p. 273). Joint attention deficits can lead to difficulties in social and communication skills, which re-quire attention to eye gaze, facial expression, and gestures.

It is easy to see that these deficits can have an enormous impact on a student's classroom participation. The need to pay attention to multiple-step directions, follow the teacher's finger pointing to the whiteboard, follow the example of your peers as they line up at recess, understand the "ANGRY TEACHER FACE" that tells everyone to get quiet ... these are but a few of the hundreds of times a day when joint attention is required at school.

Deficits in joint attention can also make peer interactions challenging. For example, there is a common perception that students with autism are uninterested in social participation with others – an assumption that is often due to deficits in joint attention. For example, I have worked with teachers who misinterpreted an absence of joint attention as a student not desiring interaction or even as having lower cognitive ability than was truly the case. This is an unfortunate consequence that can lead teachers to lower their expectations for a given student, which in turn puts limits on opportunities for the student.

Delayed and/or Uneven Language Development

Some students with autism are nonverbal or have limited verbal skills, but many children with autism have average or even advanced speech and language skills. Nevertheless, even for students who are verbal, language skills are often unevenly developed. Thus, even older students with greater verbal communication skills may have significant differences between their expressive and receptive communication (Grossman & Tager-Flusberg, 2012). For example, a student may have few expressive verbal skills but demonstrate extremely accurate receptive language comprehension. Conversely, a student may have a very advanced vocabulary but have difficulty with receptive comprehension.

Further, it is fairly common for a student to have a greater motivation to speak and develop a strong vocabulary in a particular area of interest but lack age-appropriate language for other topics of limited interest (Kluth & Schwartz, 2008). This can be perplexing for teachers, and is often misinterpreted as the student being manipulative or unwilling to talk about topics of low interest. Overall, uneven language skills can have a significant negative impact on academic performance, such as reading and content comprehension (Flores et al., 2013).

Some children with ASD do not develop functional verbal speech, so it is critical to teach and give them regular access to alternative or augmentative communication (AAC). Picture systems, voice output devices, and sign language are common alternatives to verbal communication (Stokes, n.d.). Never assume that a child who does not verbally communicate is not capable of comprehending language. For this reason, for example, it is important to remember not to speak about the child as if she were not present. Overall, it is critical for the classroom teacher to work closely with the student's speech-language pathologist to assess the child's communication needs and become proficient in communicating with the student through her preferred mode of communication.

Poor Nonverbal Communication Skills

Many students on the autism spectrum have difficulty using and understanding nonverbal communication, such as facial expressions and gestures, to give and take meaning from spoken language (Aspy & Grossman, 2008).

I was once asked to consult with a team about a student with ASD, whom I will call Brian, who had an extremely high IQ and had exceptional math and science skills but appeared to be very disengaged in the classroom. The teacher described him as frequently "zoned out" and "staring into space," even in class discussion. When I brought it to Brian's attention that the teacher thought he was bored in class, he didn't understand why.

I took photos of my face with different expressions and asked him to identify which one showed me looking angry, sad, bored, happy, etc. He could not identify a single picture correctly until he received direct instruction on visual cues to look for. In turn, I asked him to take pictures of his own face looking happy, sad, angry, bored, etc., with his favorite computer application. While he was highly motivated to do this activity, the resultant pictures showed a series of photos that were barely distinguishable from one another. When I asked him to teach me how to know he was angry, for instance, he responded with confusion. "I throw things and scream," as if this was obvious. In addition, once Brian was told that other people use nonverbal communication to express themselves and to understand what others are thinking, he had an epiphany: "So is that like when all the kids are being loud and the teacher stands with her hands on her hips and puts her eyebrows together, and then they all get quiet?" He had finally understood the universal "angry teacher look." Brian is a great example of how lack of the ability to express and understand nonverbal communication can negatively impact classroom participation.

Indeed, if you did not understand, or even realize, the presence of the powerful nonverbal communication going on around you all the time, it could easily seem to you that screaming and throwing things were the logical way to express frustration or anger. Without knowing how to use gestures, body language, or facial expressions to communicate, many children with autism have vocal outbursts, become aggressive, melt down, or throw tantrums in an attempt to make their feelings understood.

Repetitive or Rigid Language

Students with ASD may have a unique "style" of spoken communication (Aspy & Grossman, 2008). For instance, sometimes a student may seem interested only in talking about a particular topic of her choosing. This may be frustrating to a teacher when the topic of class discussion is the main idea of a reading selection and the student with ASD raises her hand to participate only to begin talking about the relative merits of Google Maps versus MapQuest.

Also, in an effort to say something appropriate to initiate or maintain a conversation, a student with autism may use the same phrases over and over. For example, a student I once knew used to ask everyone he saw (even those he did not know), "What did you have for breakfast?" This was a question that his teacher often used to start Morning Circle, and the student was simply applying what the teacher had modeled as a way to start a conversation, not realizing that this would be an unlikely conversation starter for most people.

Likewise, students may say things or repeat lines from a movie, cartoon, or commercial. While such statements may appear to be somewhat related to the conversation at hand, they are not spontaneous remarks but memorized scripts. For instance, a speech-language pathologist once asked a student where she might go to find more prizes for the classroom treasure chest, which was almost empty. The student, mimicking a popular commercial of the time, said, "Don't worry! I'll park my truck in the low-rent district and pass the savings on to YOU!" This type of communication is sometimes referred to as delayed echolalia – the student repeats at a later time a word or phrase that they have heard.

Some students repeat words immediately after hearing them, also referred to as "echolalia" (Aspy & Grossman, 2008). This can lead to misunderstandings. For instance, I once observed a very frustrated paraprofessional who was working with a young lady whom she had described as being "very verbal." During lunch, the paraprofessional would ask the student, "All done?" to which the child would respond, "All done." The paraprofessional would remove the food, but the girl would get very angry and grab it out of her hands. In reality, she didn't mean that she was "all done," she was simply echoing the words of the paraprofessional.

Limited or Special Interests

The DSM-V describes individuals with autism as having highly restricted, fixated interests that are abnormal in intensity or focus (e.g., strong attachment to or preoccupation with unusual objects, excessively circumscribed or perseverative interest) (American Psychiatric Association, 2013). Some students with autism are very verbal and able to speak at great length and in depth about a topic that is of special interest to them.

For instance, I once worked with a student who could talk in incredible detail about *The Titanic*, with vocabulary that would send me scampering to Google for clarification! However, the same student did not indicate any ability or interest in participating in a reciprocal conversation about *The Titanic*. I might say, "I saw a show about that just last month!" or would try to demonstrate interest by asking, "How many people escaped?" but he would just continue talking as if I had not spoken at all.

Social Skills Differences

Some students with ASD have significant deficits in what we think of as "social skills," mainly due to their unique combination of communication characteristics. It can be difficult to understand how someone who is highly verbal can have extreme language deficits that impact their social interactions, yet that is exactly the case for many students with ASD. Actually, the simple act of holding a conversation is not a simple act at all ... in fact, far from that. It is a highly complex skill, and for learners on the autism spectrum, it is one that must be analyzed and taught as a hierarchy of specific skills (Coucouvanis, 2005).

In order to understand the deficits in pragmatics – the study of how context influences the meaning of language – it is important to understand that many students with ASD demonstrate "mindblindness," or the inability to theorize what someone else is thinking – also called theory of mind (Aspy & Grossman, 2008).

Neurotypical individuals use theory of mind all the time to negotiate social interactions, such as understanding when someone is joking or being serious, or understanding how someone might react to certain information. One teenage boy I worked with could not understand why he was not getting a date with a young lady he was interested in until it was pointed out to him that talking frequently about his fascination with "Silence of the Lambs," a movie about a serial killer, was very off-putting to her.

Many students with ASD find this aspect of communication particularly puzzling and challenging. Indeed, to some, it is so foreign that they do not realize they have a deficit in this area. Difficulty with theory of mind can also lead to difficulty understanding what Myles, Trautman, and Schelvan (2013) refer to as the "hidden curriculum," or the unwritten rules of social interactions.

For instance, I was recently having a conversation with an adult friend of mine who has ASD. Andy was very upset because his sister had gotten angry at him for never asking about how she and her children were when he called or came for a visit. Andy said, "I don't understand why she was so angry. She said that I was selfish and didn't care about them." I explained to him that sometimes people get their feelings hurt when others don't seem to be interested in asking about them. Andy shook his head and said, "No, her feelings aren't hurt." When I asked why he didn't think her feelings were hurt, he answered, "Because I do care about her and her family and I didn't mean to hurt her feelings." It was very hard for him to understand that someone could have her feelings hurt by something he did not intend to be hurtful. He was assuming that since he cares about his sister and her family, she must know this.

Howlin, Baron-Cohen, and Hadwin (1999) pointed to some other important examples of how theory of mind can impact social communication. For instance, it is critical to monitor facial expressions, comments, and body language in order to understand and respond appropriately to what someone is communicating. We do this both when sending and receiving messages to ensure (a) that the other person understands what we are saying and (b) that we have understood correctly, and then adjust, as needed, words, gestures, and facial expressions.

Let's take a look at some of the other complex skills required for success in even the most basic social interactions.

- **We need to recognize that conversations require a clear "intent."** This is the ability to request, make comments, ask questions, protest, persuade or convince, refuse something, or perhaps negotiate a compromise. In order to be considered polite and use effective communication, we have to monitor how frequently we need to participate in conversation with a partner. If we don't speak often enough, the conversation dies, but

if we speak too much, our partner will get frustrated or bored and stop communicating with us. We have to develop the skill of keeping the conversation flowing, including taking turns and recognizing when it is our turn to speak.

- **We need to recognize how to stay on topic and when it is okay to change topics.** We pay attention to very subtle signals that one topic is coming to a conclusion and that it is okay with the other person to talk about something different. We wait for an appropriate time, and then we make some connecting comment to transition to another topic. These subtle signals are somewhat like a code that is extremely difficult for many individuals with autism to understand, yet come naturally to most neurotypical individuals.

- **We need to consider our timing.** We consider what is the right timing for discussing particular topics. We may want to talk about "American Idol" with our work colleagues, but we likely don't do it in the middle of a staff meeting.

- **We need to change our tone and the level of vocabulary we use based on the situation.** For instance, we speak differently to our friends and family than we might with our boss or a police officer. Without our finely honed predictive skills, we could end up in some sticky situations! Whether or not we realize it, we are always decoding when and how to communicate to be perceived as polite, appropriate, and "with it" socially. But these skills do not come naturally to many students on the autism spectrum and, therefore, need to be taught directly, just as surely as we must teach new reading vocabulary, a new mathematics skill, or the scientific process for problem solving.

Effect on Friendships and Bullying

"Mindblindness" can create challenges for students with ASD in making and keeping friends. For example, they may say or do things that are perceived as rude, tactless, unkind, or insensitive.

An example would be the child I once worked with whose friend came to school crying because her cat had been run over by a car. The other children gathered around the unhappy girl, patting her back, hugging her, or saying kind and comforting things. The child with autism joined in the conversation, but shared, "I saw a cat get run over once. Its guts were all over the road!" Understandably, the little girl was even more upset by this statement, though the child with autism had intended no harm.

The same characteristics that can make it difficult to navigate social situations can also make the student with autism prone to bullying. Wanting to be accepted, difficulty understanding sarcasm, and not knowing when someone is making fun of them are a recipe for disaster in a situation where another student is seeking to take advantage of the student with autism. Indeed, it is estimated that students with ASD are up to four times more likely than their neurotypical peers to be victims of bullying (O'Conner, 2012). Every classroom teacher must be constantly vigilant about identifying potential bullying, and not only preventing it but also in helping the student with autism recognize it and react in a way that effectively keeps her safe and comfortable at school.

Restricted Pattern of Activities, Interests, and Behavior

According to the DSM-V, individuals with autism demonstrate an insistence on sameness, inflexible adherence to routines, or ritualized patterns or nonverbal behavior (American Psychiatric Association, 2013). In general, most students with autism crave predictability and "sameness," and this extends to their play, their interests, and their daily routines. As a result, changes in routines or unpredictability can be difficult and upsetting for them. Indeed, disruption of routine and "sameness" is often at the root of a behavioral "meltdown." Therefore, maintaining a high level of consistency and predictability is one of the most critical types of support the general education teacher can offer. At the same time, it is also one of the most challenging, given the degree of unpredictability that is potentially present in school on any given day.

At times, teachers misinterpret a student's insistence on "sameness" as the child being spoiled, manipulative, or choosing to be difficult. However, such behavior is a core characteristic of ASD and should not be interpreted as a choice – even though the child may have developed learned behaviors in an attempt to control his environment due to a need for sameness. It is equally important to know that students with ASD can develop positive learned behaviors to deal with unpredictability, and it is an important job of all service providers and parents to reinforce these positive coping skills.

Students with ASD often have a particular interest that may be surprising or atypical for their peer group. I have worked with very young students who had an extensive knowledge of specific and in unusual topics that seemed far beyond their age to comprehend, such as how washing machines work, the engineering specs of *The Titanic*, Amish lifestyles and traditions, and the nesting habits of non-migratory birds. By the same token, I have worked with bright and high-achieving adolescent students who had interests that seemed unusual to their teenage peers, such as Thomas the Tank Engine, Disney movies, or Teenage Mutant Ninja Turtles.

Often teachers feel the need to reduce what they see as the student's "preoccupation" with a particular topic in an effort to get the student engaged in more expected ways in the classroom. However, a more productive strategy is to encourage and reinforce special interests, recognizing that they can be keys to motivating engagement and even lead to potential career options (Kluth & Schwartz, 2008.) After all, most of us have ended up in the careers and hobbies in which we excel by pursuing our special interests. It is important that the same respect and opportunities be afforded to individuals on the autism spectrum.

As classroom teachers, we know that all students benefit from consistent expectations, routines, and rules. Students with ASD have even more need for consistency and predictability than their neurotypical peers. As a result, they may exhibit unexpected behaviors as they try to create order and predictability or avoid unfamiliar situations or experiences. Unfortunately, anyone who has worked in a school environment recognizes that there is no such thing as a "typical school day." Weather-related delays, assemblies, teacher absence, construction projects, regular building maintenance ... the number of factors that can present unanticipated changes in the routine of the day are endless. While the classroom teacher cannot prevent all unanticipated changes, there are many factors that **can** be proactively planned to offer the greatest degree of predictability possible within the reality of an environment that is somewhat unpredictable by nature.

The DSM-V describes one characteristic of autism as stereotyped or repetitive motor movements, use of objects, or speech (American Psychiatric Association, 2013). When many people envision or imagine a "child with autism," they think of a nonverbal child sitting alone in a corner rocking or flapping his hands or standing in the middle of a room spinning endlessly. While some students may indeed demonstrate those behaviors, the tendency toward repetitive, restricted behaviors can manifest in many different ways than those.

Students with ASD may engage in such repetitive motor movements for a variety of possible reasons, including to block out overwhelming sensory input, to create a safe and predictable environment, to attempt to self-manage their emotional or physical state, or simply as an ingrained behavior that has been practiced for a number of years (Rudy, 2014). We all engage in some type of "stereotypical" or repetitive behaviors. You may have noticed young women who twirl their hair around their finger or a coworker who crosses his legs and then jiggles his foot when sitting in meetings.

It is important to recognize that while we all have developed such motor habits, students with ASD may have more noticeable, less expected, and more ingrained motor habits than most of their neurotypical peers. Generally, these behaviors can be expected to increase in frequency and intensity when the student is under stress or not feeling well (Boyd, McDonough, & Bodfish, 2012). Thus, the young girl mentioned above may twirl her hair more frequently when taking a test than when hanging out with her friends.

Another variation of restricted interests/repetitive behaviors is that children on the autism spectrum may play in an unexpected or atypical manner. They may be less inclined to engage in "let's pretend" type of play with other children, preferring instead to line up toys according to their attributes such as size, color, or shape. Or they may only desire to interact with a particular piece of the toy, such as spinning the wheels of toy cars and trucks (Rudy, 2014).

At times, this preoccupation interferes with productive activity. For instance, when given a set of markers to color a map in social studies class, a student with ASD may get preoccupied with arranging the markers in the order of the colors in the spectrum or may only wish to remove all the caps and then put them back on, over and over again. In these instances, teachers can plan materials proactively to remove potential distracters and/or schedule an activity so that completion of the required task is followed by some time where the student can engage with the materials in her preferred way.

Sensory Differences

One of the most significant changes to the diagnostic criteria for autism, as reflected in the latest edition of the DSM, is the specific inclusion of sensory differences. Truly, in the hundreds of students with ASD I have seen in my educational coaching work, this piece of the puzzle has proven to be especially challenging in the sensory-rich experience that is school. Once again, it is important to recognize that while the unique combination of sensory traits may vary from individual to individual, some researchers have estimated that up to 90% of students with autism have sensory abnormalities (Leekam, Nieto, Libby, & Wing, 2007).

Sensory differences can occur in any combination of an individual's sensory systems, which include:

- auditory (hearing)
- visual (seeing)
- tactile (touch)
- gustatory (taste)
- olfactory (smell)
- vestibular (balance and movement)
- proprioceptive (muscle and joint input)

(Myles, Mahler, & Robbins, 2014)

In any of these systems, students with autism may be either less sensitive or more sensitive than neurotypical peers. How a person receives sensory information, interprets it, and then reacts to it, is highly individualized. Our sensory systems help us receive information from the environment to discriminate what is around us. Sensory input gives us pleasure as we take in preferred sights, sounds, smells, touches, and movement. However, it also helps us know when we are in danger, and helps to trigger the "fight, flight or freeze" response that keeps us out of harm's way.

By helping us discriminate our surroundings and cueing us when to anticipate pleasurable experiences and when to anticipate potential danger, our sensory systems help us know how to respond in expected and effective ways as we encounter different situations. Thus, the unique way in which we process and respond to sensory information through each of our sensory systems can have a direct impact on our behavior (Myles et al., 2014).

Registration

One aspect of how we process sensory information is our "registration" or awareness level of sensory input. Some people have a low registration, or awareness level, of  certain types of sensory information, meaning that they do not notice as quickly when sensory input is present in their environment. A student with low registration of auditory information, for example, may not notice when the teacher calls out her name or gives directions to the class and, therefore, may need a visual or tactile cue that the teacher is addressing her. Other students may have a high registration for noticing sensory input and may become overwhelmed more easily by sights, sounds, smells, tastes or movement (Brown & Stoffel, 2011). For instance, a student with a high registration for auditory input may cover his ears or become upset during a fire drill or when in a noisy environment such as music class or the cafeteria. In addition to levels of sensory awareness being different to begin with, it is possible for those awareness levels to change or become more extreme under different emotional or physical conditions, for instance, when the student is under stress, upset, tired or hungry (Myles et al., 2014).

Regulation/Modulation

Another way in which people differ in their sensory processing involves whether or not they are "active" or "passive" in their approach to trying to control how much sensory input they take in. People who have an "active self-regulation style" actively try to either build in or avoid sensory input in order to stay in their optimum state of alertness and/or calm. In contrast, people who have a "passive self-regulation style" tend not to actively control how much sensory input they are receiving and, therefore, are more likely to just react to the sensory information in the environment (Brown & Stoffel, 2011).

The combination of a person's registration level (high or low) and her self-regulation style (passive or active) creates four unique types of sensory style, according to Winnie Dunn's model of understanding sensory processing:

	Low Registration	High Registration
Passive Self-Regulation	Low Registration	Sensory Sensitive
Active Self-Regulation	Sensory Seeking	Sensory Avoiding

(Dunn, 2007)

Thus, in addition to differing in how we register sensory information, we also differ in how effectively we "modulate" sensory information; that is, how effectively we attend to or ignore sensory input to keep our nervous system appropriately calm or alert and, consequently, how effectively we are able to respond in an expected manner to the sensory experience. When all of our sensory systems are working well, we are able to attend to the important information in our environment, process it efficiently, and react to it appropriately. When a student has a dysfunction in one or more sensory systems, teachers may notice it in their unusual reactions to sensory information that is present in their environment, because they (a) don't seem to notice it, (b) seem to seek it out to an unusual degree, (c) try to avoid it, or (d) react to it in an extreme way.

It is well beyond the scope of this book to describe in detail how dysfunction in each of the sensory systems may impact specific student behavior. However, it is important to recognize that up to 95% of students with autism struggle with modulating their sensory processing (Ashburner et al., 2008). Therefore, it is critical that all teachers remain ever aware that these sensory differences can have a significant impact on students with ASD and take time to speak with the occupational therapist about any sensory testing that may have been conducted with the student, so that specific supports and accommodations can be planned and implemented.

CHAPTER FOUR

Classroom Environment – Setting the Scene for Success

If you walk into 10 different classrooms, you will likely experience 10 very different environments. One classroom will be highly organized, neat and tidy, decorated with bright primary colors, printed fabric on the bulletin boards, and lots of artwork dangling from the ceiling. Another classroom will be very plain, decorated with mostly neutral colors and with only the bare minimum of information posted. Yet another room might look like a page from an *I Spy* or *Where's Waldo?* book, with decades worth of materials, books, and papers stuffed into every corner, toppling out of every bookshelf, and covering every horizontal surface.

Each of the environments will sound different, too. One classroom may be so quiet that you can hear a pin drop, the silence only punctuated by the occasional soft-spoken teacher giving instructions. Another may be a cacophony of sound ... students chattering in cooperative work, background music playing, and the teacher speaking in a loud and animated voice. Yet another may be fairly devoid of "people-created" noise but suffer the acoustic woes of an older building – echoes from concrete walls, the screech of chair legs moving on tile, and diesel truck engines and other "street noise" from the open windows.

Many factors contribute to the creation of a classroom environment. Some factors, like building age and type of construction, are largely outside of the teacher's control. For instance, many newer buildings are built to be acoustically friendlier and may be carpeted, with much less ambient auditory interference. Some buildings have built-in cupboards with doors that can enclose most materials, while others rely on a variety of shapes and sizes of shelving, cupboards, and tables to store materials in a more visible way.

However, many other factors of classroom environment are under the influence, if not the control, of the classroom teacher. While teachers create environments in which they believe their students will be most comfortable and successful, the reality is that our classroom design plan is often based largely on the environment in which we as teachers are comfortable and that motivates us to do our best work. This is understandable. It is a natural inclination to arrange and live our lives based on our own preferences and experiences. For instance, if you are a teacher who is highly motivated by visible evidence of your impact on students, you may be inclined to display lots of student work on bulletin boards, on the doors, or hanging from the ceiling. Another teacher may feel like too much student work on display distracts attention from the important reference materials that are posted in the room.

The point of this chapter is not to delineate right from wrong or good from bad. Instead, the focus will be on how various factors in the classroom environment can support or challenge a student with ASD due to the characteristics discussed in Chapter Three. Indeed, the National Standards Report on evidence-based practice for students with autism (Wilczynski & Pollack, 2009) points out that environmental structure is a well-established strategy for supporting students with autism.

In the following, we will focus specifically on five major types of environmental factors: visual input, auditory input, movement opportunities, physical conditions, and social-emotional climate. The discussion of each includes specific strategies found in the Appendix.

Visual Input

Many students with ASD rely a great deal on visual input for learning, because it tends to be their preferred learning modality. Students who process visual information more readily and more quickly than auditory information benefit from visual supports when delivering instruction (Kinnealy et al., 2012). For this reason, it is generally recommended that classroom teachers provide a host of visual supports for the student with ASD, including visual schedules, mini-schedules, written rules, learning contracts, picture cues, and even picture-based communication systems (Meadan, Ostrosky, Triplet, Michna, & Fettig, 2011).

Once a classroom is well organized, without extraneous visual clutter, the use of visual supports can be extremely beneficial for all students. Students with ASD may especially benefit from visual supports for communication, behavior support, organization, and transitions from activity to activity (Meadan et al., 2011).

Visual supports can take many forms, depending on a student's age, developmental level, reading skills, and complexity of communication. Different types of visual supports include the use of actual objects, photographs, simple drawings, and/or text. For instance, to support a student in knowing where the class is going next in the day's schedule, a student could be given an item representing that location (e.g., a lunch ticket for the cafeteria or a ball for the playground), a photograph of the location, a simple drawing that represents that location, or a printed schedule with the name of the location on it.

PLAYGROUND

In addition, visual supports are needed for various purposes, as illustrated in the following.

Purpose	Example of Visual Support
Communication	Picture choice board
Behavior Support	Sticker chart showing stickers earned for good behavior
Organization	Color-coded folders and bins for keeping and turning in homework assignments.
Transitions	A visual 5-4-3-2-1 countdown to show how much time is left before an activity ends.

Teachers use many visual supports in daily instruction because most students benefit from the static or unmoving information that comes from a visual aid. That is, when we speak to someone, the information stays only as long as we are talking or as long as the listener holds it in his memory, but visual information stays available as long as the recipient needs to reference it. This is particularly important for learners with ASD, who tend to have difficulty processing auditory information within the specific time it is being provided (Myles, Hagiwara, Dunn, Rinner, & Reese, 2004).

Daily schedules, signs, or symbols to label locations within the school, rules posters, and "to-do" checklists are just a few examples of the types of visual supports a teacher can incorporate into daily instruction for all students, but in particular for students with ASD, for whom "Visual Supports" are one of the evidence-based practices identified by the National Professional Development Center on Autism Spectrum Disorders (Hume, 2013).

Reducing Visual Clutter

Reducing visual clutter is a universally sound approach to instruction for all students, as too much competing visual input reduces the brain's effectiveness at attending, focusing on, and processing the information we need to tune in to (McMains & Kastner, 2011).

As teachers, we typically begin the school year with our rooms containing the critical information that students will need to access for a successful transition to our classroom: a "Rules" poster; fire and tornado drill directions; a calendar or morning meeting area with weather chart, 10's chart, and job board; labels for important locations, such as learning centers, etc. However, as the year progresses, we tend to continue adding visual information as we introduce new topics – the rules for "I before E" here, the water cycle poster there, a multiplication chart here, the bulletin board on how to be a good friend there.

Most neurotypical students eventually become used to the ever-increasing visual learning supports and tune them out – in essence, the visual supports become like wallpaper. The typical student rarely references most of the far-point reference materials on a regular basis. So, in reality, these supports are often not serving a purpose for these students. However, many students with ASD process visual stimuli differently, and it may either take longer for them to notice and process information (hypo-sensitive)or they may notice them much more quickly and take much longer for them to reorient their attention between competing visual information in different locations (hyper-sensitive) (Ashburner et al., 2008).

Whether students are hypo- or hyper-sensitive visually, extraneous visuals can end up competing with critical information and, therefore, have the potential to be distracting and/or overwhelming to a student with ASD. In fact, the great amount and variety of visual input can make it harder for the student to access the visual supports that he really needs in order to function, such as his visual schedule, the classroom rules, etc. A cluttered environment with too much competing visual input actually restricts the ability to focus attention and process visual information (McMains and Kastner, 2011). As a result, it may be difficult for any student to prioritize which items to pay attention to and which ones can be ignored in a visually cluttered and chaotic environment. For this reason, it is critical that the general education classroom teacher be vigilant about limiting the visual input to only the most current and necessary items that are required for the students to reference regularly.

As a teacher in a small classroom with limited space, I found a number of organizational strategies helpful:

- I kept my frequently referenced posters and charts on a flip chart so I could easily flip to them when needed rather than having them posted on the walls all the time.

- I made sure that any items that must be posted all year long (rules, tornado drill instructions, etc.) remained in the same location throughout the year if possible.

- The visual input that I posted was bordered with simple, bold borders to make it clearly distinguished from its surroundings and easy to focus on (Rapp, 2014).

- I stored as many items as possible within opaque containers or within closed drawers or cupboards when not in use.

- For materials that were hard to "contain," I found that a simple solution was to cover open shelving with draperies, curtains, or even sheets with pressure-mounted rods, shower rings, Velcro®, or hooks.

Strategies like these not only prevented my students from becoming visually distracted or overwhelmed, they also emphasized the most critical visual information for all students to reference, thereby increasing the likelihood that the entire class could find the important information they need at any given moment.

From S. Kabot & C. Reeve, 2010, *Setting up classroom spaces that support students with autism spectrum disroders* (p. 57). Shawnee Mission, KS: AAPC Publishing. Used with permission.

Creating Visual and Physical Boundaries

In Chapter Three, we discussed how important predictability and clear, concise expectations are for students with ASD. The way you structure your classroom can provide support for this underlying characteristic. For example, having clear visual and physical boundaries helps students to understand the functions and the expectations of each area of the classroom.

It is fairly simple to create boundaries with the furniture that is already in your classroom, such as desks, shelves, tables, cupboards, filing cabinets, rugs, study carrels, movable dividers, and gym mats. Visual boundaries can also be created with signs, labels, color or shape signs, placemats, carpet squares, curtains or sheets, and colored masking tape (Kabot & Reeve, 2010).

For instance, look at the following classroom layout, in which the teacher has established clear areas for different purposes.

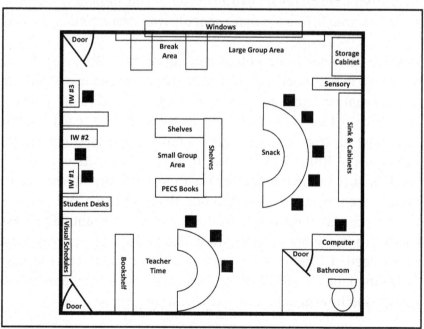

Note: Adapted from S. Kabot & C. Reeve, 2010, *Setting up classroom spaces that support students with autism spectrum disroders* (p. 38). Shawnee Mission, KS: AAPC Publishing. Used with permission.

Once an area has been defined, expectations can be established and taught for that area.

In the above layout, it is clear where the individual work stations are located. Once the students understand that this area is dedicated to individual independent work, then rules and expectations can be taught. For example: *In the individual work area, you follow your mini-schedule to do each task; You are expected to work quietly in your own area; If you have questions or need help, you put the red flag out on your desk until the teacher comes.*

Again referring to the above layout, at the top center is the "break area;" it is clearly delineated by storage cabinets. Different rules and expectations may apply to this area, such as: *No more than two people in the break area at a time. You can remain in the break area until the visual timer runs out of time. You can choose your seating option (bean bag, moon chair, or lying on the rug). You can choose any item off the shelf to do or you can do nothing. If you leave the break area before the timer goes off, your break time is finished.*

Positive behavior intervention and supports (PBIS), a systemic approach to proactive, school-wide behavior based on a response to intervention (RtI) model, emphasizes the need to not only establish consistent behavioral expectations but to teach specifically how these rules apply in different areas or settings ("Core Principles of PBIS," 2014). Thus, the critical aspects of effective visual and physical boundaries are that you maintain consistent areas once they are established and that you teach and practice the purposes and expectations of each area. This simple process can be transformative for the student with ASD, as it provides the much-needed predictability and routine and reduces the cognitive demands required to process where to go, where to find things, and how to behave in each location.

See the Appendix for the following Auto Door Openers:

- **Reducing Visual Clutter**
- **Creating Clear Visual and Physical Boundaries**
- **Providing Visual Supports**

Auditory Input

Another important aspect of any environment is the auditory input present. Think of your favorite, most relaxing place to be – your happy place. Many times, our "happy places" involve sounds that help put us in a relaxed and happy emotional state. Perhaps you envision a beach location with the sound of the waves crashing over the pier. Or you might imagine an idyllic country cottage on a quiet summer night, with the sound of crickets chirping through the open window. Sounds can have an enormous impact on our emotional state. Additionally, they can impact our ability to focus, sustain attention, and gather information (Kinnealey et al., 2012).

Nature sounds, along with certain types of music, tend to have a calming, quieting effect on our nervous system. The opposite is true for other sounds, which dysregulate us and make us feel nervous, anxious, or irritated. These sounds can also vary from person to person. For some, loud rock-and-roll music is annoying, but for others it is energizing. Many hate the sound of jackhammers on concrete when they are stuck in traffic. Some people even find the hum of an air conditioning unit or the buzz of fluorescent lights to be annoying and distracting.

As mentioned in Chapter Three, many students with ASD have sensory issues, some of them related to the way they process auditory input. Some seek out particular types of sounds. For instance, one student I know loves the comforting sound of running water and seeks it out by turning on the faucet, going to the window when it is raining, or shaking a rain stick that is available in the classroom. Other students are less able to tolerate auditory input, or certain types of sounds. For instance, I know a student who got very upset at the hum of the air conditioner in his classroom.

Many students with autism require more time to process auditory information than neurotypical students (Kwayke, Foss-Feig, Cascio, Stone, & Wallace, 2011). While most teachers are aware of the importance of giving any student sufficient "wait time" to process information, this is especially important for students with ASD. I have worked with many students who could give brilliant responses in class if only given the time to process the question. Sadly, I have seen many students miss out on the opportunity to "show what they know" due to lack of opportunity to process and then respond.

For the same reasons that it is helpful for most students if you reduce visual clutter, it is important to reduce "auditory clutter" within the general education classroom. Students who are hyposensitive to auditory input and, therefore, seek that type of stimulation may have difficulty noticing and attending to important auditory information, like instruction, directions, and behavioral redirections. Conversely, students who are hyper-sensitive to auditory input are easily overwhelmed and stressed by too much sound. Finally, students who have difficulty processing auditory input quickly may become frustrated when too much auditory input comes in at once. The bottom line is that most of us have more difficulty processing auditory information in a noisy environment.

Auditory clutter can take many forms within a classroom. Ambient noise can include the buzz of the overhead lights, the hum of the heater, the street noise from cars and trucks going by, playground and hallway noise, student chatter, the small talk among staff members, computer sound, and more. Such noises can be distracting or even stressful to students who are hyper-sensitive to sound and can mask what sounds are critically important to attend to for students who are hypo-sensitive to sound. Having a quieter classroom allows fewer distractions while allowing students to more clearly perceive when auditory input needs their attention.

Reducing Auditory Clutter

A number of researchers have delved into the auditory sensory differences of children with ASD, particularly the negative impact of classroom noise on the learning and attention of students with auditory hypersensitivity (Ashburner et al., 2008; Kinnealey et al., 2012; Myles et al., 2014). Additionally, research has shown that students with autism may have difficulty reorienting between visual and auditory stimuli (Ashburner et al., 2008). For these reasons, it is helpful to try to reduce overall auditory noise levels and build in individualized opportunities for additional auditory input through headphones, personal or classroom amplification systems, listening centers, etc., for students who need it to succeed.

Some of the simplest ways I have found to reduce auditory clutter in the general education classroom include:

- **Consider teacher voice volume.** As a teacher, recognize that your volume and tone of voice influence the overall noise in the classroom. You may have noticed, for instance, that teachers who speak in a quieter voice tend to have quieter classrooms for the simple reason that the students have to keep their voices at a lower volume in order to hear the teacher. Conversely, as the teacher's voice increases, she tends not to become more audible because her students respond by becoming louder as well. So speaking in a quiet voice is a good start to reduce the overall noise level of your students.

- **Monitor and limit unnecessary adult conversations.** It has been my experience that it is easy for auditory clutter to develop exponentially with each adult staff member in the room. Staff members such as teachers, paraprofessionals, and therapists tend to tune one another out and underestimate the amount of personal conversation that goes on between and among them. It is a good idea to video- or audiotape your classroom occasionally and check to see how easy it is to distinguish teacher instructions from the other ambient noise in the room.

- **Include sound-absorbing items in your classroom design.** Some newer school buildings are carpeted and have acoustically designed ceilings and walls. In older buildings, area rugs on tile or wooden floors can help prevent echoing sounds in the classroom. Simple fabric panels stretched over wooden picture frames on the walls can also absorb sound. In addition, it is very helpful to have one or two flexible, folding gym mats in the room that may be set up on edge to create an acoustic barrier around a student's desk if he is distracted by extraneous noise. The gym mat absorbs some sound as well as providing a barrier to visual activity in the room.

- **Teach students to control voice volume.** Another simple way to design a quiet and calming classroom environment is to teach all students guidelines for self-managing their voice volume. When I was teaching, I used a stoplight with red, green, and yellow light bulbs for noise management in my room. I taught my students that when the red light was on, it meant that I should be the only one speaking unless a student was called on. When the yellow light was on, it meant that quiet conversation was allowed while the students were working in partners or groups. When the green light was on, it indicated free time or that social conversation was allowed. This became a quick and easy way for me to help students and staff quickly identify what level of conversation was allowed. Teachers who do not have an actual stoplight can create a laminated poster of a stoplight with removable red, yellow, and green circles to indicate voice volume expectations.

- **Practice what volume of voice can be heard at different distances.** I often combined this with a measurement lesson in math class. We would get out rulers and yardsticks and practice what volume of voice could be heard at a 6-inch distance from each other, at 12 inches, at 3 feet, etc. Then all students and staff had a point of reference for volume so that I could say, "You may work in partners. Please use a 6-inch voice," and the students knew the expectation.

- **Provide "whisper phones" for students to read aloud or talk to partners.** I provided small, straight segments of PVC plumbing pipe as "whisper phones" that students could use to speak to their partners through when working together so that the sound was contained between partners. Curved PVC "elbow joints" were available as individual "whisper phones" for students who needed to read out loud in order to process what they were reading. This allowed them to read aloud into one end of the pipe, and it would go directly to their own ear, allowing them to speak more quietly but still hear their own voice.

 See the Appendix for the following Auto Door Opener:
- **Reducing Auditory Clutter**

Movement Opportunities

An important aspect of any environment is the movement going on within that environment. Consider for a moment your preferences when driving. If given the choice, would you prefer to drive 50 miles on a congested interstate with cars going at high speeds, cutting quickly in and out of your lane and occasionally ending up in dead-halt traffic jams for long periods, or would you prefer to travel those same 50 miles on a wide, lightly travelled two-lane highway, where you can go a consistent speed and rarely even have to tap the brakes? If you are going shopping to find a special gift for someone, would you prefer navigating a crowded mall on Christmas Eve with hundreds of people pushing and shoving as you try to find what you want amidst disorganized clearance displays, and then stand in long lines to pay, or would you prefer to shop at your own pace, leisurely browse well-organized aisles and then quickly pay for your selection and be on your way?

Similarly, patterns of movement in the classroom can make that environment more or less conducive to learning. In classrooms there seems to be almost non-stop movement of students searching for the Kleenex box, taking the most circuitous route possible to the pencil sharpener, hovering near a friend's desk on the way to turn in their homework, or standing in a long line at the teacher's desk waiting to turn in lunch money or ask a question about an assignment. However, there are classrooms in which the majority of students are seated unless they have a specific purpose for moving and the room is arranged so that even a total stranger could ascertain within moments the location of all the most critical resources, materials, and functions in the room.

The Role of Peripheral Vision

The purpose of our peripheral vision is to make us quickly attuned to movement coming from either side, and thus it is processed by our brains to alert us (Bayle, Henaff, & Krolak-Salmon, 2009). As a result, the more unpredictable movement that is present in the classroom environment, the greater the chance that students become distracted or feel "on guard" or highly alerted to the visual stimulation that movement creates. This is particularly the case for some students with ASD who have a more sensitive peripheral vision system and/ or higher levels of anxiety regarding potential unexpected tactile input that may be signaled by movement from either side (Doman, 2006). Thus, while not all students may have an "on-guard" response to peripheral movement, limiting unpredictable movement/moving visual input helps students who do have a sensitivity in that area, and at the same time it does not harm any other student.

Movement around us can cause anxiety if we do not enjoy the anticipation of potentially being bumped into, touched, or otherwise having our personal space invaded. While some students with ASD enjoy and seek out tactile (touch) input, others have tactile defensiveness, which can create stress around unpredictable movement in the environment and the resulting anticipation of unexpected contact from others (Cara & MacRae, 2013). All of us have different levels of comfort with touch from others. Some of us touch and receive touch with little or no hesitation, offering hugs, pats on the back, handshakes, and high fives as a method of greeting, encouraging, celebrating, or comforting. Others are more aptly described as "hula hoop" people, who prefer a perimeter of personal space around them. We may be fine with a hug if we initiate the contact or from those who are very close friends or relatives, but we may feel uncomfortable with uninvited or unpredictable touch from others.

Many students with ASD exhibit this same tendency but to an even greater degree. Again, while some students with ASD may enjoy and seek out touch, it is easy to build in additional opportunities for touch for those students who enjoy that, through a box of fidgets, manipulative learning tools, and sensory play areas like rice bins and water tables, even within an environment that limits unpredictable movement for the other students who may not enjoy it.

Establishing Clear Movement Routes

A number of simple strategies can assist in creating a classroom with consistent, efficient, and non-interfering movement patterns that support student success. A well-planned classroom has obvious and easily accessible paths for moving from location to location so that students can access the necessary materials, follow the expected procedures, and avoid interfering with the learning of others as they move about the room. Key locations that will be accessed by all students on a regular basis, such as the mailboxes, cubbies, tissues, "turn in" trays, computers, and learning stations, can be planned so that they are accessible via clear, efficient routes that don't interfere with individual student work areas.

Preventing Unnecessary Movement

Measures can also be taken to prevent unnecessary movement. First and foremost, teach and let the students practice the expectations, or the "traffic rules" of the room. Rules vary according to the grade level, the room arrangement, and the purposes of movement in the room.

To prevent multiple students having to travel through the classroom, the following ideas may be helpful:

- Provide each student with a flag or table tent to put up on their desk when assistance is needed, and then one of the adults in the room can circulate to give assistance.

- Place a "parking lot" poster with a pad of sticky notes in a corner for students to post non-urgent questions that can "wait," such as "When are the field trip permission slips due?"

- Keep materials like scissors, glue, crayons, etc., in caddies on student tables or near each student group to prevent students from having to travel to retrieve and replace these items throughout the day.

- Schedule Q/A (Question and Answer) time periodically throughout the day and teach students that questions should be jotted down and asked at that time.

- Teach students to ask nearby students first before going to the teacher for simple questions.

Building in Movement Opportunities/Breaks

Just as movement can be visually and tactilely troublesome for students with ASD, other students have difficulty standing or sitting in one spot for long periods due to difference in their vestibular (the system that regulates movement and balance) sensory systems. For example, some students have great difficulty understanding where their body is in space and feeling wobbly or dizzy, as they sense a lack of equilibrium when standing for long periods of time without touching something to ground them, such as leaning against the wall. Such students find seemingly simple classroom expectations, such as standing in line waiting for the restroom or navigating the middle of a crowded hallway, extremely challenging.

One simple universally effective way to build movement into a student's day is to allow the student to do his work in various positions that incorporate natural movement (Rapp, 2014). For example, depending on the student and the task at hand, students may stand on a rocker board, sit at their desk on an air-filled cushion that moves, sit with a clipboard in a rocking chair, or sit on a physio ball or T-stool. This allows students to receive more input through their vestibular systems to maintain comfort and alertness. (Consult with an occupational therapist for the most suitable solution.)

Both the vestibular and proprioceptive (body awareness or input from joints and muscles) sensory systems of all students may also be effectively supported when teachers incorporate movement breaks into the day. Movement breaks can be highly beneficial for all learners to remain in the "ready" zone for learning (Jensen, 2005). That is, movement opportunities allow students to remain alert enough to stay engaged but calm enough to pay attention and focused.

Some teachers assume that this means that a large chunk of instructional time must be traded for exercise sessions or extra recess, which is often not realistic in these days of high-stakes testing and high levels of accountability for academic outcomes. But the reality is that short movement breaks can easily be incorporated into instructional activities and as transitions between activities and locations throughout the day without any significant interruption in instruction.

In choosing activities for these short breaks, proprioceptive movement is usually considered "deep pressure" or "heavy work," involving activities that give input to muscles and joints.

Examples of simple, quick proprioceptive movement breaks that most students can do without any special equipment include:

- seat push-ups
- desk push-ups
- wall push-ups
- hand squeezes
- calf raises
- lunges
- squats

Another good option for movement breaks is to choose activities that are linear and vestibular in nature. (Think of "vestibular" movement as anything that changes the position of the students' head and "linear" as meaning in a straight line, back and forth, or side to side.) Linear vestibular movement can provide a quick and simple "wake-up" opportunity for students periodically through-out the day (Davis & Duble, n.d.).

Examples of quick and simple vestibular movement breaks include:

- "head-shoulders-knees-and toes"
- boat rowing with a partner
- jumping jacks
- touch toes
- hopping or skipping in place

If the schedule permits, a simple yoga session embedded during the day can offer the best of both worlds – proprioceptive and linear vestibular movement in one! A short series of yoga poses prior to lunch (yoga is best performed on an empty stomach), for example, can help "reset" the students for the remainder of the day. Under Recommended Resources, I have included resources for simple yoga routines that can be implemented in the classroom. If you have any questions about how to implement a yoga program in your classroom, consult a motor specialist or certified yoga teacher to ensure safety and effective implementation. Also, all students should be cleared by their physicians for safe participation in a yoga program.

For a simple calming routine, students can be taught to breathe in and out through the nose, counting to 3 on the inhalation and to 6 on the exhalation while performing the poses. Having the students hold each of these poses for three breaths would be an excellent mid-morning, before-lunch, or mid-afternoon break that should help all students stay calm and focused for the afternoon. If your students are young, you can build movement breaks into the day by having students "animal walk" to their various locations: bunny hopping, elephant walking, bear walking, etc. If your students are older, you may choose to build movement into the actual lessons or assignments by incorporating kinesthetic tasks such as role play, skits, demonstrations, nature walks, and charades.

As always, consult your school's occupational therapist for recommendations of vestibular and proprioceptive movement options for individual students.

 See the Appendix for the following Auto Door Openers:
- **Reducing Unneccesary Movement**
- **Providing Frequent Movement Breaks**

Physical Climate

Each of us has specific preferences for the physical environment in which we are most comfortable with regard to temperature, lighting, and scent. All of these factors have a great impact on our comfort level, and sometimes even our availability to participate (Kinnealey et al., 2012).

Temperature

I have worked with many students with ASD who become uncomfortably warm in an environment that feels comfortable to me and other students. By the same token, some students have the opposite reaction. Being too warm can result in stripping behaviors, removal of shoes, or seeking cool surfaces, such as lying down on the cool tile of the hallways or bathrooms to seek relief. For this reason, it is important to understand that some students may need to dress in layers at school or have different clothing options available so that they are able to either add or subtract items of clothing to adjust for temperature differences.

In older buildings that do not have efficient or consistent climate control, these issues can be greatly exacerbated. In some cases, it may be helpful to have icepacks or cool water readily available for students who are over-heated.

Lighting

In addition to temperature, lighting can have a significant impact on our mood and our comfort in a given environment. When my husband and I shopped for homes, we both responded well to the home we ultimately chose for the same reason: across the back of the house, the living room, kitchen, and family room are each bordered by sliding glass doors. As a result, the house is

flooded with light much of the day. For me, a good deal of natural light is essential to productivity and alertness. In fact, that is such an ingrained part of my internal makeup that it never occurred to me that anyone else had a different experience with light!

For a close colleague of mine, however, light has a very different effect. My friend wears sunglasses at all times when in bright natural light. While she does prefer natural light to fluorescent light, any kind of direct bright light causes her great discomfort.

Some research (Kinnealey et al., 2012) indicates that children with autism demonstrate an adverse reaction to fluorescent lighting, including increased stress, more repetitive behaviors, and more learning and behavioral challenges than when learning in an environment with more natural lighting.

It has been my experience as well that, while some students with ASD seek out lights and colorful objects and enjoy that input, many others have a higher degree of light sensitivity and prefer less direct light. Therefore, I advise teachers to plan their general environment around the needs of those who are hyper-sensitive to light and then build in individual opportunities for those who seek light and color through increased lighting in their work area, or preferred toys, objects, and activities that provide extra visual/light input. Examples of items that may provide extra input for students who desire light include toys that light up and computer/tablet apps that light up with bright colors.

While the general classroom lighting must be sufficient for all students to be able to see their work and avoid eyestrain, natural or incandescent lighting is preferable to many students when possible (Rapp, 2014). Many new buildings offer the option of turning banks of lights on and off in different areas of the classroom. This allows greater control of the overall level of lighting in the room by offering the option to darken a small area for students to take a break from the light occasionally while allowing students who benefit from more lighting to work in the brighter areas. Another simple solution is to use fire code-approved magnetically attached fluorescent light covers that can filter the light. These are made in a variety of colors by a number of manufacturers, including Educational Insights and Learning Resources, and may be purchased from many occupational therapy equipment companies but also major retailers such as Staples and Amazon.

Smell

Our sense of smell is processed very quickly and has a quick route to our amygdala, which causes our sense of smell to have a strong connection to our emotions (Krusemark, Novak, Gitelman, & Li, 2013). So, for good or bad, the smells that surround us impact us very directly and with great intensity. Many students with ASD and many neurotypical students have differences in their sensitivity to smell, and the particular smells that are preferred or non-preferred can vary greatly (Myles et al., 2014).

Therefore, when designing your classroom environment, it is wise to strive for a neutral environment with regard to scent. Avoiding scented air fresheners, candles, and heavy lotions and perfumes will help keep the environment comfortable for most students, especially those whose olfactory system is sensitive. For hypo-sensitive students who seek out and enjoy smells, additional smell input can be built in for them individually based on their preferences by letting them use preferred lotions or even by spraying a preferred scent on a handkerchief or wrist band that they can keep with them.

 See the Appendix for the following Auto Door Opener:
• **Creating a Comfortable Physical Climate**

Social-Emotional Climate

A less quantifiable but no less important factor in the creation of an effective environment for learning is the social-emotional "feel" of the classroom. What goes into making you feel "at home" somewhere? Likely, you feel most comfortable in a place where you are surrounded by people who treat you with respect and kindness and who seem to genuinely like you. On the other hand, you likely feel nervous and on edge in an environment where you don't know anyone or where you are concerned that you might be made fun of, or not fit in.

All students need to feel safe from bullying or humiliation and have a sense of belonging to be productive and successful in class. All students feel uncomfortable, nervous, or uncertain at times. However, for students on the autism spectrum, this sensation can be greatly magnified by the social, behavioral, and communication differences that are part of the autism diagnosis. For this reason, it is important to foster a climate of tolerance, acceptance, respect, and support among classmates. This can be accomplished by formal lessons, team building games, class-wide positive behavior support systems, and other specifically targeted strategies, but perhaps the most critical factor is the teacher's own modeling of the expected attitudes and behaviors.

One of the best things teachers can do to foster a sense of well-being in the classroom is to manage their own emotional "mindset." Sousa and Tomlinson (2011) discuss the critical "mindsets" that guide a teacher's behaviors and interactions, which, in turn, have a tremendous impact on their classroom's social-emotional climate. According to Sousa and Tomlinson, components of the mindset of "effective" teachers include:

- They realize that they have a lifelong impact on their students.

- They believe they must make their classrooms a safe and secure place for all students.

- They believe that all students want to and can succeed.
- They believe that the social-emotional needs of students must be addressed.
- They are empathetic and try to view things through their students' eyes.
- They believe in helping students feel ownership of their own learning.
- They believe in building on students' individual strengths and areas of interest.
- They support an environment where there is no fear of making mistakes or being humiliated.
- They view discipline as a teaching process, not a system of punishment.

(Sousa & Tomlinson, 2011, pp. 19-21)

When teachers come from this mindset in creating their classroom climate, they ensure that their students have the opportunity to demonstrate their talents, grow from their mistakes, develop confidence and persistence, and learn the skills to contribute in a positive way to their classroom and community.

While the social-emotional climate of a classroom is critical to all students, it is important to recognize that students with ASD have particular and unique challenges in this area, which will likely demand special planning and attention. Thus, emotional vulnerability is one of the associated characteristics of autism that can have a significant impact on their daily lives. Some of the emotional differences they cite include:

- tendency toward stress and obsessive worry
- appearing sad or depressed
- appearing anxious

- exhibiting rage or meltdowns
- self injury
- suicidal comments
- difficulty tolerating mistakes
- low frustration tolerance
- low self esteem
- negative self talk
- difficulty identifying, expressing and controlling emotions
- difficulty understanding others' emotions
- difficulty managing stress.

(Aspy & Grossman, 2008, p. 19)

Because of their emotional vulnerability, it can be very difficult for some students with ASD to feel comfortable, supported, and successful in the complex social systems present in the classroom (Ochs, Kremer-Sadlik, Solomon, & Gainer Sirota, 2001). Many students with ASD with whom I have worked over the years have poignantly expressed their feelings of being outsiders or that they don't belong or are not well accepted by peers and/or teachers at school. For this reason, it is especially important to take extra steps to ensure that these students are welcomed, encouraged, and supported by teachers as well as peers.

Some teachers and parents find it helpful to educate peers about autism so that they better understand and can more effectively support their friends with ASD. This must be done carefully and with sensitivity to the feelings of the student and with regard to the age and development level of all students in the room.

At times, it is helpful and beneficial for the student with ASD to be involved in educating his/her peers. I worked with two fifth-grade students and their guidance counselor to create a Power-Point presentation about autism and about its unique impact on each of them, which they subsequently presented to the entire fifth grade of their elementary school. They even created a pre- and posttest, collected data on the impact of their presentation, and shared it in a poster session at a national teacher conference. It was a very empowering experience for those two young men, although many students might not enjoy such a public experience. (I must share that when we finished presenting, both boys were very excited and feeling happy and proud about the experience. I asked them what their favorite part of the experience had been, and after much thought, much like many typical 11-year-old boys, they admitted that the most fun part was riding the escalators up to the food court in the convention center!)

Teachers are well advised to collaborate with the student's parents, counselors and/or therapists, and any others who might have meaningful insights into how best to create a safe and comfortable climate for them at school. I have included a number of resources for teaching students about autism in the Recommended Resources section in the Appendix.

Clearly, the emotional vulnerability aspects of autism can dramatically impact opportunities to develop friendships as well. Therefore, this is another area that is of utmost importance when planning for successful inclusion of students with autism. Social relationships make up a huge part of the school experience, and students with ASD need specific support, instruction and guidance on social skills in order to feel successful in participating in your general education classroom. Some of the recommended strategies for supporting social skills, which we will discuss next, can also be helpful to many or most other students (Rapp, 2014).

Many well-researched and evidence-based instructional approaches are available to help students with autism be successful in navigating the complex social environment of school. For example, social narratives are stories or scripts that can be used to teach students about the social expectations of various situations (Myles et al., 2013). Social narratives can take many forms, but all of them have the goal of providing the cues and skills needed to participate successfully in various social situations (Myles et al., 2013). I have included a list of commonly used social narrative approaches in the Recommended Resources section in the Appendix.

 See the Appendix for the following Auto Door Opener:
• **Providing Social-Emotional Support**

CHAPTER FIVE

Elements of Instruction

While specific lesson plan formats vary from school to school, most of the models are based on the same fundamental components. For the purpose of discussion in this book, I use Madelyn Hunter's lesson planning format (Hunter, 1976). It has been the basis for many other planning formats through the years and is still in common use in many school districts and teacher preparation programs with some variations.

In this chapter, we will first look at the general elements of effective instruction and then present some special considerations that will help you adapt those elements to make them accessible to the students with ASD in your classroom. Let's start with a review of Hunter's recommendation for lesson planning.

Hunter's Model for Lesson Planning

1. **Objectives & Standards:** The teacher should know what OBJEC-TIVES and STANDARDS of performance are expected, and the pupils should be informed about these objectives and standards.

2. **Set:** The purpose of this element is to "get" and "focus" student attention to the lesson. The teacher literally attempts to create receptive minds.

3. **Teaching:** This element includes the components of input, modeling, and checking for understanding. Each of these components can incorporate a multitude of methods and techniques.

4. **Guided Practice:** This is an opportunity for students to grasp and develop the concept through participation in activity or exercise. This element is most effective if students are continuously monitored for the purposes of time-on-task and assessment of learning. Immediate feedback (peer or teacher) is powerful at this point in the lesson.

5. **Closure:** The purpose of this element is to help students "bring things together in their own minds." Closure allows the brain to secure the "parts" of the concept or skill as a "whole." It's similar to the experience of stepping back and gazing at the whole picture when the final piece of a puzzle is in place!

6. **Independent Practice:** The primary purpose of this element is to reinforce the content or skill that was mastered in the lesson. Independent practice of the concept or skill should continue over time and be applied to as many relevant situations as possible. In other words, independent practice should include use of the concept or skill in a context other than the one in which it was learned.

From http://sps.k12.mo.us/sd/elements.html

Objectives and Standards

Most general education teachers are familiar with and supportive of the philosophy that all students must be held to the same high standards and that high expectations are essential for all students, including those with disabilities, to meet their potential. So, in general, it should be assumed that if a student with an ASD is placed within the general classroom for instruction, she will likely be working on the same standards and objectives as the neurotypical students within that classroom. Nevertheless, the objectives and standards may need to be differentiated to allow all students access to the information in a manner in which they can be successful.

Many schools incorporate a response-to-intervention (RtI) model (Bradley, Danielson, & Doolittle, 2005), wherein behavioral and academic supports are provided in a tiered fashion with some supports available to all students, more intensive supports provided to targeted groups of students with similar needs, and even more intensive, individualized supports provided to students who are identified as needing highly specialized instruction or behavior support. RtI can be greatly enhanced by taking a "UDL" perspective and understanding that when instruction is carefully planned, many of the students' needs are effectively addressed through the general instruction with less need to remove students for remediation or alternate instruction. Thus, good universal design of instruction is the foundation of an RtI model.

Differentiating Instruction

Differentiating content involves first assessing students' level of knowledge with the content so that students can be flexibly grouped for instruction according to readiness for any new learning. This does not mean that students are in fixed learning groups for all subjects all day long, but if the pre-assessment reveals that there are gaps among students in the class in terms of their readiness for a particular piece of content, all students will be introduced to that content at an appropriate entry point (Tomlinson, 2001a).

Think of instruction as a large stadium with multiple entry points. Recently I was at a baseball game in a large ballpark. Take a look at the map of this impressive stadium:

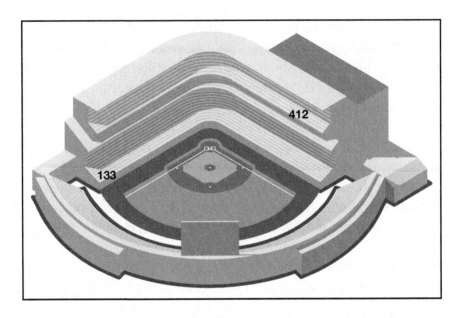

When we arrived at the stadium, we entered at the ground level near section 133, on the lower left of the picture. Our seats were in section 412, in the section near the upper right of the map. Since we had not visited the stadium for many years, the first thing we did was to look at the stadium map to get a general feel for the layout of the venue, read the signs over the entry ways, and if we had questions, we located a stadium usher to confirm that we were headed in the right direction. We knew that such a large stadium would have multiple entry points and methods of getting spectators to their appropriate seat quickly and efficiently and that there were resources and methods in place to assist us in getting where we needed to go. In other words, there would be no point in us wandering the aisles of the stadium, pushing past fans in their seats, getting hot and tired and cranky before the game even began.

Our "pre-assessment" of the situation allowed us to move quickly past entry points that would not take us where we needed to go, get to an escalator that took us quickly and easily up to the nose-bleed section for which we had purchased tickets, and then navigate quickly to the seats assigned just to us so that we arrived in time to see the first pitch thrown out. Similarly, as Tomlinson (2001a) points out, pre-assessment of content to be taught allows you to be the usher for your students, guiding them to the optimum location for them to participate in instruction.

 See the Appendix for the following Auto Door Opener:
• **Assessing Readiness**

Set

Every teacher has his or her opinions about which element of instruction is the most critical and could likely make a good case for each one. When I am teaching, I spend the most energy and time on "set" because I find that if I don't get my students engaged from the get-go, every other step will be a struggle. Plus, planning an effective "set" is the fun part of lesson planning for me – How will I get students' attention? How will I keep them engaged? How will I make sure they remember this lesson a year from now?

While all students need engaging and motivating instruction, students with ASD present unique challenges in this regard, including their difficulty with sensory modulation, central coherence, executive function, and theory of mind, as well as communication and social differences. In addition, their motivation to participate can be impacted by their tendency towards very restricted or specialized interests (see Chapter Three). One of the most frequent frustrations of general education teachers when teaching students with ASD is their difficulty initiating and maintaining engagement, especially in non-preferred topics or tasks. Let's take an example.

I once observed a fantastic student teacher who had a talent for developing a good set, but completely failed to engage her student with autism. She was teaching a reading lesson on the critical thinking skill of "prediction." She was using the wonderful picture book *The Mitten* by Jan Brett. Before reading the book to the kindergarten class, she gathered all the students on the carpet and took out from behind her back a large knit mitten that was obviously stuffed with items. This alone was fascinating to the majority of students, who began clamoring about, drawing closer and closer to the teacher, and asking a million questions. While she had to shush and redirect all the excited little bodies, her student with ASD never even noticed the mitten and was sitting quietly brushing the fibers of the carpet square on which he was seated, first all in one direction and then in the opposite direction. As the teacher read the story, she paused occasionally to pull an item from the mitten and let the children guess what would happen next in the story. However, the student with autism never even looked up to see the mitten and therefore, didn't notice what was so intriguing to the other students or engage in the learning activity of making predictions. He was fascinated instead by the changing color and pattern that appeared on the carpet when he brushed it in different directions. He obviously also greatly enjoyed the tactile input that the brushing provided.

Due to a failure to recognize those characteristics, the teacher misinterpreted him as being unmotivated, when actually he was just differently motivated. The more important concern was that his differences in motivation prevented him from learning the valuable skill being taught in the lesson. For this particular student, who was so motivated by the feel of the carpet under his fingers,

it may have been highly motivating for him to sit by the teacher and hold the mitten, which would have provided him some tactile input and would have brought him "into" the activity through his preferred modality. For the majority of students an effective set is enough to motivate their participation or at least their passive engagement in the instruction. However, for students with autism, the general education teacher may need to connect the "set" or "hook" of the lesson to a preferred topic or activity to finally engage the student.

 See the Appendix for the following Auto Door Opener:
- **Incorporating Students' Special Interests and Activities**

Teaching

This element of instruction – teaching – is the aspect that is the most obvious when people think of what teaching is. It is the part where the teacher provides information, models the skills he wants the students to demonstrate, and checks to see if the students understand what is expected of them. This is where it is critical to have a solid understanding of teaching pedagogy, including strategies for incorporating different learning modalities, multiple types of intelligence, and different levels of Bloom's taxonomy (1956) within the lesson, to ensure that it is comprehensible and appropriately challenging and motivating to students. First, let's briefly review some of those critical concepts to good differentiated instruction.

Learning modalities refer to the different systems through which students taking in new learning. Some of us learn better by hearing information, some of us prefer to learn through seeing demonstrations or examples of what we are to do, while others feel the need to get their hands involved and DO something before they really feel they understand it.

When differentiating instruction, it is also critical to consider different *"types" of intelligence* (Sousa & Tomlinson, 2011). The most well-known model for understanding the different types of intelligence is Howard Gardner's "multiple intelligences model," which he proposed in his 1983 book, *Frames of Mind: The Theory of Multiple In-*

telligences (Gardner, 1983). Gardner suggests that rather than being quantified with a single IQ score, intelligence is better represented by understanding that people have different proclivities in different types of intelligence, which he sums up in these categories: verbal linguistic, logical-mathematical, visual-spatial, musical-rhythmic, bodily-kinesthetic, interpersonal, intrapersonal, and naturalist (Gardner, 1983).

Sousa and Tomlinson point out that in the multiple intelligences model, it is generally regarded that most of us work within all those categories of intelligence, but that almost all people have preferences and strengths in some areas over others (Sousa & Tomlinson, 2011). This relates to instruction in that teachers need to plan instruction that incorporates opportunities for students to learn and demonstrate knowledge through a variety of those learning preferences in order to engage all students who have very diverse learning profiles.

Finally, *Bloom's taxonomy* refers to a framework outlined in *Taxonomy of Educational Objectives* (Bloom, 1956), which explains different levels of cognitive complexity in learning. It begins with the most basic levels of comprehension and moves up through application of learned information to new situations, then to analysis of the learned information, then on to synthesizing the information into new ideas, and finally being able to use the learned information to evaluate and make judgments. While this taxonomy is taught in beginning teaching pedagogy, it is helpful for teachers to keep in mind that instruction needs to encompass all of those levels of understanding for all students in order for them to maximize their learning potential.

Just as we all have preferred learning modes, teachers also have preferred teaching styles. Not surprisingly, since I am a person who enjoys a great deal of discussion, I tend to use the Socratic method, teaching a great deal through lecture, guided questioning, small-group discussion, and verbal problem solving. But even though I prefer to teach and learn that way, I have to incorporate visual supports and more hands-on and movement-based learning activities to ensure that all of my students are actively engaged.

An effective teacher designs instruction that incorporates many learning styles and types of intelligence through the course of a day, a week, a year. Not all styles are present in each lesson, but over the course of time, each type of student will experience some instructional activity that allows him to "shine" in his preferred modality in the classroom of a teacher who truly understands universal design for learning – instruction is not a matter of designing a "one-size-fits-all" lesson but of using flexible, customized instructional methods and materials that can be easily tailored to the needs of individual students.

A proactive approach to better understanding the learning styles and types of intelligence represented in a class as a whole involves spending the first few days of school in some fun and motivating pre-assessment activities designed for the students and teacher to get to know one another. Learning centers can be created to let the students take simple self-assessments on learning styles, multiple intelligence, interests, and talents. It only takes a few hours to compile the results of these "orientation" activities into some charts that can be used to guide instructional planning for the entire school year.

In the university courses I teach, students spend the first class taking a number of self-assessments to help me get a picture of the learning characteristics of the class. Once the students have completed profiles on their learning styles, multiple intelligences, etc., I compile the results into a chart so that as I am planning my lessons, I can reference how important it is for me to provide visual supports or interactive discussion, for instance.

I once had a class where 80% of the students came out as very visual learners. With that class, I always made sure to provide a Power-Point handout outlining the lecture. However, the same semester I taught the same class to a different group of students who were very auditory and came out on the multiple intelligence assessment as about 80% in the "interpersonal" category of intelligence. That group would have been bored to tears by endless PowerPoint lectures; they needed lots of discussion and group work. Of course, I planned some of both types of instruction for both groups, but I adjusted the emphasis to meet the needs of each unique class.

This component of Hunter's model – the "meat" of instruction – will be more explicitly explored in the coming chapters on multiple means of representation, expression, and engagement.

 See the Appendix for the following Auto Door Opener:
• **Conducting Student Orientation**

Guided Practice

One of the most overlooked or undervalued aspect of instruction is guided practice (Rosenshine, 2012). This element is critical because it allows the teacher to watch the student perform the skill that has been introduced and then, as appropriate, give instructive feedback designed to prevent the students from practicing mistakes. For students with autism, this is particularly important because of their tendency to develop ingrained patterns of behavior (see Chapter Three).

When we think of guided practice, we might think of listening to a student read aloud and giving her prompts or cues to use the decoding strategies we have taught, or perhaps we think of giving students some math problems to do on the whiteboard, where we can observe how they solve problems and give feedback throughout the process. However, beyond academics, it is just as important to give students guided practice in social and behavioral skills that are expected to be practiced in the school environment. For example, just as students cannot learn mastery of multiple-step division without guided practice and opportunities for feedback, neither can they be expected to master the complex and often unwritten rules of social interaction. For students with ASD, due to their underlying characteristics of social, communication, and behavioral differences, these skills require guided practice and instructive feedback every bit as much or even more than many academic skills.

For instance, I observed a teacher working with a pair of students who were fighting over whose turn it was to read in a shared reading activity. They had been instructed to take turns, reading paragraph by paragraph aloud. The student with ASD enjoyed reading aloud and was very angry whenever the other student tried to begin his turn reading. The teacher decided that next time he gave a shared reading assignment, he would give all the student pairs a checklist in which each paragraph had been numbered and instruct the students to sign their initials next to the number after their turn was over to show that they had each done their part and no one else's part. If he walked past during the activity and saw that one student had not had the chance to initial any of the paragraphs, he gave a reminder and asked why only one student's initials were on the checklist so far.

This little bit of feedback throughout the activity helped remind the students of the expectation and was enough to support the student with ASD in the collaborative turn taking that was part of the lesson. Additional strategies for using guided practice effectively include the following:

- Implement guided practice as a safe time for students to practice skills without being graded and without negative consequences for mistakes.

- In general, do not move on to independent work until students demonstrate 80% mastery during guided practice.

- Schedule individual conferencing time with students periodically to discuss progress on long-term projects.

- Jot comments on sticky notes rather than writing on the student's paper or just placing an X by incorrect items. The remove-ability of the sticky note emphasizes the importance of correcting the work and that the comment is not a "final" assessment of the work.

- During guided practice, set a timer to cue "checkpoints" at which students check their work with a neighbor and raise their hand for your assistance if they have questions.

- Let students "teach" the concept to you or to other students so you can assess their understanding of the processes involved.

Closure

The closure aspect of instruction refers to the stage when the teacher brings all the "pieces of the puzzle" together for students, helping them to understand how the skills they have just mastered fit into the larger context of their learning.

One of the cognitive characteristics of many students with ASD is difficulty with "central coherence" (Aspy & Grossman, 2008). Central coherence refers to our ability to form meaningful links over a wide range of learning experiences and generalize what we have learned over a wide range of contexts. Many students with ASD have "weak" central coherence; that is, they tend to learn discrete or rote skills well but may have extraordinary difficulty deriving the "main idea" or the larger concepts from those isolated skills (Collucci, 2011). For instance, the student with ASD may be able to remember literal, discrete details of a reading passage, but have difficulty in comprehending what the main idea was.

I observed a middle school student in a seventh-grade language arts class recently. The class was reading the book *Hatchet* by Gary

Paulsen about Brian, a young boy who has to learn to survive on his own in the woods after a plane accident. The teacher was leading a discussion on one of the final chapters, in which the main character finds a survival pack on the plane but is saddened because he realizes that using the items (such as freeze-dried food and tools) would remove his interdependence and harmony with nature, which he has grown accustomed to and satisfied by through his many trials.

A student with ASD was able to describe in great detail each item in the pack and even what it would be used for. He could also identify that Brian was sad, since that was explicitly stated in the chapter. However, when the teacher asked why Brian might feel sad as he looked through the items, the student could not put together the big picture, which was the main point of the events. His answer to "Why do you think Brian feels sad?" remained very literal and focused on the details, such as "Because he has a rifle" or "Because he has freeze-dried food."

The closure of the lesson is an opportunity to reinforce those larger ideas and help students organize what they have learned, prioritize it, put it in context with other lessons they have learned, and know how this knowledge will be useful to them in the future. In the case of the student who was having difficulty understanding *Hatchet*, the teacher led the class in completing a T-chart on the whiteboard. On one side, it listed difficulties that Brian encountered and, on the other side, things that he learned to love, that were positives about the experience. Then, to help the students apply the bigger lesson of the story (sometimes adversity results in personal growth), she asked each of the students to complete a T-chart about an experience of their own that had been difficult but had resulted in good things.

The student with ASD wrote about coming to the middle school. On one side of the T-chart, he listed all of the things he had been afraid of: people he didn't know, hard classes, not knowing how to open his locker, etc. On the other side, he listed the good things he had experienced: a new best friend, not having to go out on a playground any more, getting to go to the library after lunch each day, etc. This activity is a great example of "closure": helping students draw the learning experience to a close and understand how it applies to their own lives and to their future learning.

While many teachers, myself included, tend to rush through the closure process, it is an important process and one worth putting a bit more thought into than just asking students to summarize what they have learned or reviewing it in a *Jeopardy*-style game at the end of the week. After all, even if we teach a highly motivating, standards-based lesson incorporating all the learning styles and giving loads of opportunities for guided practice, if the students are not able to integrate what they learned into their skill set and know how and when they can use it, the effectiveness of the lesson is greatly diminished.

Good closure to a lesson can include:

- Reviewing the key points of the lesson
- Giving students opportunities to draw conclusions from the lesson
- Describing when the students can use this new information
- Previewing future lessons
- Demonstrating students' problem-solving process
- Exhibiting student learning
- Creating a smooth transition from one lesson to the next lesson

This may be accomplished through a wide variety of activities, such as group presentations, class performances, art projects, skits, field trips, or cooking activities. The options for creating an engaging and memorable lesson closure are limited only by the imagination of the teacher.

See the Appendix for the following Auto Door Opener:
• **Supporting Central Coherence**

Independent Practice

In the best of all instructional worlds, there would be no "beginning" and "end" to any lesson – lessons would seamlessly lead from one to the next as students integrate their new knowledge into previously learned skills and then apply them from that point forward to a wide variety of situations and experiences. Too often, however, teachers get caught in the unfortunate cycle of feeling pressured to "get through" first this unit and then the next unit before testing time, and in the process begin to adopt a "Well, now THAT'S over with!" attitude about our teaching and learning.

While we know that is not optimal, it is absolutely critical to the concept of universal design that we look at teaching and learning as a never-ending process that we are adding to and maintaining continuously throughout our lives. That is the purpose of independent practice. Once we are satisfied through the process of guided practice and closure that our students have mastered the content we covered in our teaching, we need to consciously plan opportunities for students to independently apply those skills in new and novel ways.

Transfer and generalization can present one of the biggest challenges in teaching students on the autism spectrum (Freschi, 2006). Because of the weak central coherence discussed earlier, it can be hard for these students to see how the skills they have learned can be applied to other, novel situations. For this reason, successful inclusion of students with ASD requires planfully offering many opportunities for students to revisit, practice, and apply mastered skills periodically in new situations throughout the year.

See the Appendix for the following Auto Door Opener:
• **Supporting Transfer and Generalization**

CHAPTER SIX

Multiple Means of Representation

As described in the overview of universal design for learning, "multiple means of representation" is related to the many different methods through which information can be conveyed to students in order for them to gain the fullest understanding possible from the experience. The three guidelines recommended by CAST (2011) to enhance the use of multiple means of representation are as follows:

Guidelines for Providing Multiple Means of Representation
Guideline 1: Provide options for perception.
Guideline 2: Provide options for language, mathematical expressions, and symbols.
Guideline 3: Provide options for comprehension.

CAST. (2011). *Universal Design for Learning Guidelines, version 2.0.* Wakefield, MA: Author.

Perception

The first and perhaps most intuitive strategy for providing options for perception of information is to understand and address all learning styles within the majority of lessons taught. Tomlinson (1999) points to the importance of understanding that each student has a unique learning profile, including preferred learning activities. The more varied activities and modalities we use for instruction, the better chance we have of engaging all of our students, including those with ASD.

Another simple way for the general education teacher to provide options for perception is to use technology when presenting information. To accommodate auditory perception, for example, technologies allow for improved/enhanced perception, including classroom amplification systems, personal amplification systems, closed captioning on videos/TV, and speech recognition software, which can then translate the teacher's voice to text to be displayed for students who have difficulty understanding the spoken word or processing it quickly (Rapp, 2014). Technology can also be used for the written word; for example, allowing for easy adjustment of various elements, such as font size, volume of sound, and print contrast, to accommodate sensory and sensory and learning style differences (Hall et al., 2012; Rapp, 2014).

When incorporating options for perception for students with ASD in the general education classroom, it is important to remember that many of these students demonstrate relative strengths in their visual modality and less preference for receiving instruction through their auditory system. Therefore, it is almost always a good idea to provide visual representations of information to support and supplement auditory instruction (Meaden et al., 2011). As discussed in the section on visual supports, pictures, graphs, charts, and videos are all examples of ways to represent information visually to support comprehension of instruction, which can then be available as needed for reteaching and reference by those students who need it.

Language, Mathematical Expression, and Symbols

All students, but particularly students with ASD, who sometimes have uneven language development, may have difficulty interpreting nonliteral symbols, expressions, figures of speech, multiple meanings, and content-specific language – language that is specific to a particular subject or lesson. For instance, a math lesson is likely the only time in our lives when we will hear or use words like "addend" or "subtrahend." A geography lesson is likely the only context in which a student is exposed to the words "latitude" and "longitude."

Most neurotypical students pick up the meanings of these terms from the context in which they are presented in the lesson, but some students, including students with ASD, benefit from having an opportunity to learn these terms prior to the lesson so that they are not trying to comprehend new terminology and apply it at the same time.

For one kindergarten student that I worked with, his teacher used a song and dance to introduce each new letter of the alphabet. The song often introduced interesting or unusual words that started with that letter, which most of the neurotypical students found funny and entertaining. However, it was very frustrating to the student with ASD to have a new piece of vocabulary to figure out at the same time he was trying to master the movements of the dance. If he had never heard the word "penguin" or seen a penguin, for instance, it was hard for him to hear that new word, watch the teacher model how a penguin walked, and also learn to imitate that movement all at one time. However, once his paraprofessional began to take a few moments before the lesson to take him aside, and teach him the new words with visual aids to show him what they meant, he enjoyed the activity much more and participated successfully.

While this is a common characteristic of students with ASD, it is important to note that many neurotypical students also find these aspects of instruction confusing. Clarification of the symbols, language, and expressions used in instruction will help students to have better access to instruction and support the needs of students with autism as well. The simplest way to provide this type of clarification is to preteach the vocabulary, symbols, or expressions that will be used within the lesson.

I once heard a teacher tell a story about a fourth-grade girl who was struggling as she attempted to complete a practice assessment in preparation for the statewide assessments in her grade. As she rubbed her temples in frustration and wrote nothing, the teacher finally touched her gently on the shoulder, encouraging her, "Bethany,  you can do this problem! We have done problems just like this every day for the past couple of weeks and you know just what to do!" The confused student replied, "No, I recognize the type of problem, but it says to 'Dee-Ter-Mine' the solution, and I don't know how to 'Dee-Ter-Mine' anything ... I just know how to get the answer."

This is an example of how unfamiliarity with a specific term masked the child's actual content knowledge. If she had been pre-taught that "determine" is another word for "figure out" in a math problem, she would have been able to find the correct answer without difficulty. Students need to be exposed to multiple ways to understand the language around the learning, the assignments, and the assessments of the content being taught.

Strategies for ensuring students are familiar with critical symbols and vocabulary include:

- Preview vocabulary in standardized tests and jot down commonly used "question" or "direction" words on popsicle sticks. Keep them in a jar, and when you are asking questions in class, pull out a popsicle stick and phrase your question with that word so that students become familiar with its use. For example, if you say, "Tell me what happened in the story," pull out the word "summarize" to remind you to say, "Summarize what happened in the story." In this way, you ensure that students are familiar with terms they may encounter on tests.

- Have students maintain a notebook that is a self-created dictionary and/or thesaurus of commonly used terms on assignments and tests. They add to it throughout the year when you introduce new terms that mean the same thing as some other term. This will serve as a resource for students so that, when they come to a term in an assignment or test that they don't know, they can look it up to see, for example, that "determine" means the same thing as "solve" or "figure out."

- Have students develop flip books made of index cards on a snap ring as a resource to remember commonly used symbols and their meanings. As new symbols are introduced, have students draw the symbol on one side of an index card and an example or definition of the symbol on the back. Have students create and add index cards as new symbols are introduced throughout the year.

- If students use computers, tablets, or smartphones in class, teach them how and encourage them to look up unfamiliar words online or in dictionary or thesaurus apps.

- Since not all students have the same knowledge and experience with words and concepts, instead of having "one size fits all" vocabulary lists for new stories or chapters, have students scan the new reading material and create their own list of unknown words to look up and define. Expand to include a scavenger hunt where students interact with each other to get definitions from each other.

Comprehension

Finally, students need multiple opportunities and strategies to understand and deeply comprehend the information being taught. Comprehension of new concepts relies on a number of factors, including background experience, linking new learning to previously mastered concepts, being able to think critically and manipulate information in new ways, and applying the information in novel situations. Students with weak central coherence may require additional time spent on the integration, transfer, and generalization of information, since they may be better at rote memorization than at applying the information in novel ways or getting the bigger picture (Freschi, 2006).

For instance, at the end of a lesson on "greater than and less than" in math class, most of the neurotypical students will be able to go on and use that information to determine if the answer to a subtraction problem makes sense, because the answer should not be MORE THAN either of the numbers in the problem. A student with autism, on the other hand, may not make the inference and transfer that knowledge to the new skill of being able to assess the "reasonableness" of his answer on the subtraction page the next day.

 See the Appendix for the following Auto Door Openers:
- **Providing Options for Perception**
- **Providing Clarification of Symbols, Expressions, and Language**
- **Providing Options for Comprehension**

CHAPTER SEVEN

Multiple Means of Expression

Learners come to the classroom with varying means of expressing what they know. In this chapter, we will be discussing the common characteristics of students with ASD that can have a great impact on their ability to show/express what they have learned.

We have all had experiences in life where we knew what was expected of us, had the necessary knowledge, but had a hard time showing it. In the past months, I have been working toward my certification as a yoga instructor. I have worked hard to learn all the asanas (poses), proper breathing techniques, and correct alignment. There are a couple of poses that I am simply not able to perform due to the structure of my anatomy. But I can do approximations of the poses. I perform the pose with the assistance of props. I can recognize the appropriate or incorrect alignment of someone else doing the pose. I can describe the pose. I can draw the pose. In other words, there are many ways for me to show what I know about the pose without having to demonstrate it myself.

The same should be true in our classrooms. There are almost always multiple ways for a student to express what he has learned, and he should not be limited in his ability to participate based on a physical, communication, sensory, or executive function deficit. The CAST website (www.cast.org) recommends three guidelines for supporting multiple means of expression.

Guidelines for Providing Multiple Means of Expression
Guideline 4: Provide options for physical action.
Guideline 5: Provide options for expression and communication.
Guideline 6: Provide options for executive function.

CAST. (2011). Universal Design for Learning Guidelines, version 2.0. Wakefield, MA: Author

Physical Action

Providing options for physical action is for some teachers a more obvious and more imperative accommodation than some of the other guidelines. This is because most everyone can relate to being physically unable to perform a certain function. Maybe you were the child who couldn't get to the top of the climbing rope in P.E. class. Maybe you run 8 miles a day and are extremely fit but sit out the electric slide or the macarena at wedding receptions because you are always one step off. At the very least, most of us would hold a door open for an elderly person with a walker, or pick up a dropped billfold for a person in a wheelchair.

The point is that physical limitations are usually easier for us to identify with, since they are visible. However, we sometimes oversimplify what various factors can support or impede someone's physical participation in our classrooms. Removal of physical barriers by keeping a clean, uncluttered classroom is an important factor, but it can be just as important to support physical participation by adjusting expectations for speed, rate, timing, range of motion required, and even neatness of things like handwriting. Technology can create many options for physical participation through the use of keyboarding, touch screen choices, voice-to-text software, and switch devices.

Students with ASD may or may not have obvious physical disabilities, but ASD is a neurological condition and is almost always accompanied by some biological and sensory differences that can greatly impact physical participation in the general education classroom. For example, a student who has tactile sensitivity may require additional personal space.

Further, students with autism often have deficits in fine- and gross-motor skills, including:

- balance difficulties
- resistance to/difficulty with handwriting
- poor handwriting
- poor motor coordination
- slow writing
- deficits in athletic skills
- awkward walking gait
- unusual body posture, movements and facial expressions
- difficulty starting and completing actions.

(Aspy & Grossman, 2008, p. 18)

Clearly, these characteristics can make physical participation difficult, especially when combined with the task demands of new or difficult academic material. In addition, as mentioned, some students are easily overwhelmed by sensory input, which can greatly interfere with their ability to participate in challenging academic activity.

Think about your own ability to balance your checkbook. Few adults enjoy that task, but for most of us it is not difficult in terms of the academic or the motor skills required. However, if you were required to sit on a bar stool in the middle of a crowded department store at holiday time, holding your calculator, your pencil, your checkbook, and a bank statement on your lap and THEN try to perform the task, you may have a considerably more difficult time than if allowed to do the task in a quiet, spacious area with all of your materials within easy reach and with plenty of time to perform the task and check your work. In short, our physical participation is impacted by many visible factors but also by factors that may be less obvious.

Expression and Communication

Communication factors that can impact a student's ability to express what she has learned are often much less obvious to teachers than physical factors but may have just as much or more impact on successful participation. The basic assumption of many teachers regarding students with ASD is that if a child is verbal, he is capable of expressing himself and should be held to the same standards as neurotypical children. But communication is far more complex than simply knowing how to say words. Communication is understanding and being able to express things both verbally and nonverbally through gestures, facial expressions, and other types of body language. Communication involves understanding figurative as well as literal speech. It is understanding the many rules of reciprocity, such as taking turns, not "filibustering" on a single topic, not saying offensive things, staying on topic, and many more.

Being able to express what you know in the classroom often requires a number of social task demands as well, such as working in cooperative groups, negotiating differences of opinion in discussion, dividing out areas of responsibility, and demonstrating tolerance for less preferred activities. As we have previously discussed, these are all areas of difficulty for most students on the autism spectrum and can greatly impact their ability to successfully convey their degree of knowledge, especially on a non-preferred topic or task.

An example that comes to mind is a student I once observed who was twice exceptional: he had Asperger Syndrome and was gifted, especially in science. He had a low tolerance for discussions among his peers who did not have as high a degree of understanding as he did. Often, he understood the content better than the teacher and got very frustrated when she did not explain something completely or accurately by his standards. He was prone to slapping his forehead and exclaiming, "OH MY GOSH, REALLY?!" when the teacher or a peer would venture a comment or question that he deemed stupid or ill informed.

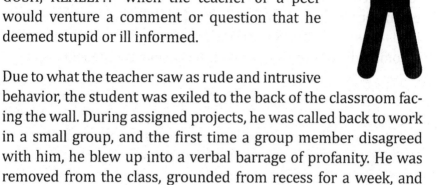

Due to what the teacher saw as rude and intrusive behavior, the student was exiled to the back of the classroom facing the wall. During assigned projects, he was called back to work in a small group, and the first time a group member disagreed with him, he blew up into a verbal barrage of profanity. He was removed from the class, grounded from recess for a week, and received an F on the assignment even though he likely had a very thorough understanding of the material.

Generally, I recommend separating behavioral and academic expectations and consequences. While this student clearly needed to learn that his explosive behavior had consequences and be held accountable for learning how to handle his frustration, it is important to recognize that this is an entirely separate and challenging type of curriculum for the student with ASD, and that he would need instruction and support in this area just as much as for any academic skill.

Thus, in reality, this student had double the task demands of the other students in the group, who had long ago mastered these social and communication skills. His communication deficits had not only earned him a week of missed recesses, they had also prevented him from expressing his academic strength. Had he been able to complete an alternate independent assignment, he likely would have been able to demonstrate mastery of the academic content. Options or alternate assignments could have included doing a PowerPoint presentation on the topic, video taping himself performing and explaining the experiment, or doing the project with a single peer rather than four.

The ultimate goal is for every student to master the skills needed to participate in all classroom activities. For this reason, it is important to ensure that all students receive exposure, instruction, and guided practice with the collaboration and social skills involved in these kinds of assignments. Students who are struggling may benefit from accommodations or modifications for certain assignments.

Accommodations are simply changes to how you offer the instruction or how you allow the student to respond, such as allowing the student to listen to reading material rather than reading it or scribing a written assignment rather than writing it.

Modifications, on the other hand, are actual alterations to what content the student is expected to learn. Examples include shortened spelling lists or different and easier learning objectives for a social studies unit. Whenever possible, consider the least alteration possible to allow the student to successfully participate. Extensive modifications to learning objectives or alternate assignments should only be offered as *options* while group work skills are still emergent, so that the student's difficulty with social skills or cooperative group skill deficits do not prevent successful demonstration of their academic knowledge in the meantime. In addition, it would have been helpful to give him instruction and options for expressing his frustration more productively the next time.

In the above example, the team was able to support the student by allowing him to practice cooperative partner work in a separate office area with a hand-selected partner whom he enjoyed working with. He was given a cue card to remind him of acceptable phrases to use when he disagreed with his work partner and was instructed that he could ask to go get a drink of water if he became frustrated and needed a break. Once he had become adept at disagreeing without losing his temper with one partner, he began practicing with multiple and varied partners, while still using his cue cards and his water breaks.

Executive Functioning

Another area that may potentially impact a student's ability to express what she knows is executive function (Aspy & Grossman, 2008) – such mental processes as the ability to organize, prioritize, self-manage multiple demands, deal effectively with impulses, plan ahead, and make logical choices.

Have you ever known someone who seemed to juggle a million different roles and responsibilities effortlessly at the same time? Maybe you are one of those people who are able to grade a pile of essays, cook dinner from a recipe on your iPad, play fetch with the family dog, answer your kids' homework questions, and balance the checkbook all simultaneously from your command center, otherwise known as the kitchen counter. Or maybe, conversely, you are the type of person who needs to get dinner started and then go into a quiet office space in your home, grade your papers with the door closed to keep the dog out, then come out and finish dinner preparation, and only after you've had some time to digest your food be prepared to tackle your son's Science Fair project. Alternately, you may be a person who just stares at the to-do list, totally overwhelmed, and decides to go play Solitaire or surf Facebook for an hour and then looks up at the clock and realizes it's 8:00 and calls the pizza place on the corner.

The point is that we all have different degrees of executive function skill, and we need to recognize that in order to successfully manage our responsibilities. We don't all have to have the same style, but we do have to learn how to support our individual style. For some people, like me, making lists is helpful so that I can look back and see what I have accomplished as I cross things off. But for some folks, looking at a list of a hundred things is overwhelming. My husband likes to write his "to-do's" on individual sticky notes and then throw them away as he accomplishes them so that they are visibly GONE. While he finds that very satisfying, I can't do that because then I worry later, wondering if I really DID that thing or just THOUGHT about doing it. This is why we need to provide multiple options to support individual executive function needs.

Technology offers many innovative and efficient options for supporting executive function. Many of us benefit from smartphones, iPods, or iPads, which allow us to have our email instantly available so that it doesn't "stack up" and become overwhelming. For me, this is a lifesaver, as I enjoy being able to address an email here and there rather than facing a list of 50 unopened emails at one time. Others do better if they save them all and set aside a half hour for opening email once a day at their desk at work.

There is no "wrong" way to approach executive function tasks as long as the student's system is functional and effective for him. However, many people do need assistance in finding the right way to organize and prioritize tasks and manage time. Students with ASD, in particular, struggle greatly with these aspects of classroom participation (Coyne & Rood, 2011). It is common and understandable that teachers tend to set up executive function supports that reflect their own preferences for managing things. But these supports may not be effective for every student in the class, just as my running "to-do" list technique would be annoying and distracting to my husband, and his sticky note technique would cause me great anxiety.

Students with ASD often respond better to visual means of managing their executive functions than auditory, if for no other reason than the visual input remains available as long as needed, whereas auditory information comes and goes (Myles et al., 2004). When given a set of multiple-step directions verbally, for instance, that information comes and goes. Students in your classroom who have a strong auditory learning style may need that verbal explanation, but students who are more visual learners may forget the instructions, become confused or anxious trying to keep it all in memory, or simply shut down from frustration.

When possible, provide visual supports, which will give all students options for revisiting expectations as frequently as necessary through strategies such as written directions, Smartboard demonstrations, color coding, and/or iPod or iPad, productivity apps. There are many excellent apps developed specifically for supporting students with autism. The list changes and expands almost on a daily basis due to the ever-changing technology landscape. Regular Internet searches of "autism apps," "visual supports apps," or "organization apps" will yield links to current and cutting-edge options at a variety of price points.

 See the Appendix for the following Auto Door Openers:
- **Providing Options for Physical Action**
- **Providing Options for Expression and Communication**
- **Providing Options for Executive Function**

CHAPTER EIGHT

Multiple Means of Engagement

By now, you are probably recognizing that there is a theme to this "universal design" business. Since we are all unique learners, we need a variety of approaches to learning/teaching on a daily basis in general education classrooms. We have talked about providing variety in how we present information and in the options available to students for expressing what they know. But one of the greatest challenges for teachers is keeping students motivated and engaged.

By simply providing multiple means of representation and expression, we have already made a positive impact on student engagement. After all, it is pretty hard to stay motivated and engaged if you cannot perceive what is being taught and/or if you have no means to express your questions or comments, and show your mastery of the subject!

Let's pretend that you have taken a once-in-a-lifetime trip to France and decide to enroll in a cooking class so that when you return home you can continue enjoying some of the wonderful cuisine you tasted during your vacation. You get to the class and find that everyone is speaking French, including the instructor. While you can speak enough French to ask where the bathroom is and how to get back to your hotel, you cannot keep up with these fluent native French speakers. The entire first class is a lecture on the basics of French cooking. The instructor stands at the front of the room and hands out detailed notes (in French) on various basic cooking techniques. This instructor is obviously very passionate about her subject; she is animated, apparently peppering her lecture with humorous stories, as the students around you laugh uproariously from time to time. She also invites questions and encourages discussion, but you must sit on the sidelines, trying to pick up a tidbit here and there but largely remaining clueless about what is going on. You have no way to interact or ask questions. While you are a pretty decent cook and have excellent questions or even insightful suggestions to add to the discussion, you have no way to communicate your knowledge.

How likely is it that you will stay motivated and engaged in this scenario? Even though you have high intrinsic motivation for the subject, without access to instruction in a mode that you can perceive and comprehend, and without any way to interact and express yourself, there is not only little motivation to participate but really no opportunity, even if you wanted to.

Had the cooking class begun with a cooking demonstration of some basic techniques, with a clear explanation of the vocabulary involved, and had you been able to try your hand at those techniques, had you been able to sample the foods from the demonstration, and had you been given a French translation app on your iPod or iPad to allow you to ask questions, would you have been a tad more motivated and engaged in the lesson? Yes, absolutely.

In the same way, without question, if you practice the Auto Door Openers suggested in the previous chapters for offering multiple means of representation and expression, you are well on your way to promoting active and positive engagement of your students. However, there are some other important factors involved in maintaining engagement, especially for students on the autism spectrum.

Guidelines for Providing Multiple Means of Engagement
Guideline 7: Provide options for recruiting interest.
Guideline 8: Provide options for sustaining effort and persistence.
Guideline 9: Provide options for self-regulation.

CAST. (2011). *Universal Design for Learning Guidelines, version 2.0.* Wakefield, MA: Author.

Interest

We know that we learn best what we have a strong need or desire to know. So you won't find me hanging out in the garage when my husband figures out how to replace the broken light on his motorcycle, because I don't have any interest in motorcycles and I don't ride. However, you may very well find me hanging out in my son's room while he changes the strings on his guitar, because I have recently started to play and I'll need to change the strings on my own guitar some day. It is only natural that we don't have equal interest and motivation in learning all subjects every day. And yet, we teachers often speak of students "not being motivated" as if motivation were a single, all-encompassing descriptor as simple, static, and absolute as eye color.

The fact is that motivation for learning ebbs and flows according to many factors: our interest in the subject, our physical wellness on any given day, our level of skill with the activity, and our reason for needing to know the content, to name just a few. For students with ASD, this can be particularly challenging due to the restricted interests and activities that are hallmarks of the condition.

To be successful in recruiting the engagement of all of our students, we must plan our instruction to be relevant to the age levels and interests of our students (Tomlinson, 2001b). Our anticipatory set, or "hook," in any lesson plan should pique the curiosity of our students and provide them with the reason why the content could be helpful or useful to them. We can also offer a variety of opportunities for autonomy in exploring facets of the topic that may be of particular use or interest to individual students (Tomlinson, 2001b). For instance, if we are teaching a group of sixth-grade students about the concept of "writer's voice," rather than having all the students write on the same topic to demonstrate their own "voice," it might be more relevant and interesting for the students to self-select a topic to write about. If students are to do a book report, giving them the choice between a traditional report, a diorama, a skit, or a musical rap to summarize the key points of the book will likely recruit the engagement of more students, including students with ASD.

Finally, but possibly most important, learning involves risk taking, and in order for students to feel comfortable taking risks, the climate of the classroom must be one of mutual support, kindness, and emotional safety. Students need to feel that their individuality will be accepted and respected and that their efforts will not be laughed at, dismissed, or shamed (Lavoie, 2007).

Effort and Persistence

Of major interest to me are the differences in the persistence and resilience among students. We have all known students who struggle terribly and fail time and again but always manage to get back on the proverbial horse and try again. Conversely, we have also had students who become discouraged and give up or become argumentative or shut down at even the most innocuous corrective feedback.

The ability to maintain effort differs among students, but having clear objectives and frequent opportunities to receive positive and constructive feedback, as well as being able to track progress is critical to supporting students in sustaining effort (Schunk, 1983). Most of us have at some point in our lives tried to lose a few pounds. What is the first thing we do? We get on the scales or get out the measuring tape to assess our current state. Then we implement whatever regimen we have chosen and periodically check our progress to see if we are making headway. If we don't have any way to see that we are headed in the right direction, it is hard to stay encouraged, especially if the diet we are following is difficult for us and we are struggling to comply with it. Many times, people find it helpful to draw a graph or chart to mark their progress periodically. It might even be helpful to indicate various points at which we will reward ourselves with a movie night, a shopping trip, or a weekend get-away to celebrate accomplishing our goals. Similarly, many students who struggle with persistence, including students with ASD, benefit from monitoring their progress toward completion of their goals, along with anticipated breaks for preferred activities or incentives for success in order to maintain motivation and effectively maintain effort (Rafferty, 2010).

Self-Regulation

We expect students to develop intrinsic motivation to be good students, behave well, complete their work, etc., but for some students, especially those with ASD, intrinsic motivation develops later or only for very restricted interests and activities (Stewart, n.d.). For these students, it is critical to set up a system that provides them the necessary social and communication supports and allows them to see a meaningful and rewarding reason for persevering through difficult tasks.

However, while it is important to help students develop these extrinsic supports, it is important to support them in their emergent self-management skills. Students with ASD, and many others, may not have the knowledge, insight, or experiences to self-manage their emotions, choices, and behaviors. The art of self-reflection, goal-setting, and making positive and productive choices in reacting to difficulty are all important skills that will impact lifelong student success as much as any academic skill.

See the Appendix for the following Auto Door Openers:
- **Recruiting Interest**
- **Sustaining Effort and Persistence**
- **Supporting Self-Regulation**

Now that we have a general understanding of some of the biggest challenges facing students with ASD in the general education classroom and have discussed a variety of supports that can be universally helpful for all of our students, you may be left wondering how it all fits together as you plan to support your student with ASD in the general education classroom. In the next chapter, we will explore a planning process for connecting the characteristics of individual students with the universal supports that will most likely benefit them.

CHAPTER NINE

Planning for Success

In the previous chapters, you have learned the basics of universal design for learning and the common underlying characteristics of ASD. Armed with this information, you now have the ability to plan your general education classroom to maximize the success of every student in your class, including students on the autism spectrum. Contrary to the assumptions of many teachers, meeting the needs of learners on the autism spectrum does not have to involve only elaborate separate interventions for individual students and does not have to detract time, energy, or effort from the nondisabled students in the class. The very supports that enhance the school experience for students with ASD will likely benefit the majority of students in your class.

Before you begin planning your classroom design, let's review some of the potential barriers to success for students with ASD.

Common Barriers to Success for Students With ASD	
Visual Clutter	Frustration With Task Demands
Auditory Clutter	Inability to Communicate Effectively
Inconsistent or Unclear Rules	Low Motivation
Chaotic Classroom Layout	Limited Opportunities to Practice Skills
Disorganized Materials and Resources	
Unpredictable Activity and Movement	Single Modality Instruction (e.g., lecture only)
Long Periods of Waiting or Down Time	Overreliance on Paper-and-Pencil Tasks
Sensory Overload	Confrontational Interactions
Social Anxiety	Limited Options/Choices

While this is not a comprehensive list, it does represent many classroom characteristics that can have a negative impact on students with autism but that can also limit learning opportunities for most students with disabilities and many nondisabled students as well. The Automatic Door Openers presented in the Appendix are surefire ways to remove these barriers and open the door to limitless learning for all of your students.

On the following pages, you will find a planning chart to help guide your classroom planning. Across the top are listed some of the most common categories of characteristics of students with autism that can impact success in the general education classroom. Down the left-hand side of the chart are listed categories of strategies that we call Automatic Door Openers because they can open the door to learning for all students in your classroom. You will find X's in the cells of the chart under the characteristics that the "door openers" can effectively support. You can look at this chart as a quick reference to find which Automatic Door Opener QuickTip Sheets to pull out of the Appendix for ideas.

PUSH TO OPEN PLANNING GUIDE

Automatic Door Openers	Characteristics of ASD						
	Communication Differences	Social Differences	Restricted, Repetitive, and Stereotyped Patterns of Behavior, Activities, and Interests	Weak Central Coherence	Mind-blindness	Executive Function Deficits	Sensory/Biological Differences
Reducing Auditory Clutter	X			X		X	X
Reducing Visual Clutter	X			X		X	X
Creating Calming Sensory Input			X				X
Creating Clear Visual and Physical Boundaries	X					X	X
Incorporating Opportunities for Learning Social Skills	X	X	X	X	X	X	X
Teaching and Incorporating Self-Management Skills	X	X	X		X	X	X
Reducing Unnecessary Movement							X
Providing Frequent Movement Breaks			X				
Providing Visual Supports	X	X		X	X	X	X
Communicating in a Crisis	X	X			X		X

Automatic Door Openers	Communication Differences	Social Differences	Restricted, Repetitive, and Stereotyped Patterns of Behavior, Activities, and Interests	Weak Central Coherence	Mind-blindness	Executive Function Deficits	Sensory/Biological Differences
Creating Purposeful Movement Breaks							X
Creating a Comfortable Physical Climate		X	X				X
Providing Social-Emotional Support	X	X	X	X	X	X	X
Using Positive Behavior Supports		X	X		X	X	
Assessing Readiness	X	X		X		X	
Incorporating Students' Special Interests and Activities	X	X	X	X	X	X	X
Conducting Student Orientation	X	X		X	X	X	X
Supporting Central Coherence	X			X		X	
Supporting Transfer and Generalization	X	X		X	X	X	
Providing Options for Perception	X	X	X	X	X	X	X

Automatic Door Openers	Communication Differences	Social Differences	Restricted, Repetitive, and Stereotyped Patterns of Behavior, Activities, and Interests	Weak Central Coherence	Mind-blindness	Executive Function Deficits	Sensory/ Biological Differences
Providing Clarification of Symbols, Expressions, and Language	X	X		X	X	X	
Providing Options for Comprehension	X	X		X	X	X	
Providing Options for Physical Action	X						X
Providing Options for Expression and Communication	X	X	X	X	X	X	X
Providing Options for Executive Function	X			X		X	
Recruiting Interest	X	X	X	X	X	X	X
Sustaining Effort and Persistence	X	X	X	X		X	X
Supporting Self-Regulation		X				X	X

How to Use the Push to Open Planning Guide

You can use the planning guide in a number of ways.

1. First you may use it to decide which Automatic Door Opener QuickTip Sheets will give you the most "bang for your buck." To do this, you might review the planning guide to see which Door Openers have X's under all of the underlying characteristics categories.

   Likely, the Door Openers in these categories will have a broad positive impact on the design of your classroom for all learners. This may be a good starting point if you are feeling overwhelmed by the process of redesigning your classroom and instruction.

2. Another way that you can use the Push to Open Planning Guide is to simply reference it as you encounter barriers to working with your students on the autism spectrum. For instance, if you have a student who is exhibiting difficulties with executive function, such as disorganization, difficulty prioritizing or completing tasks, or managing time, you could go back to the Push to Open Planning Guide, find which Automatic Door Opener categories apply, and then reference the related QuickTip Sheets for ideas on how to support your student.

3. You can also use the blank Push to Open Planning Guide as a discussion guide for the IEP team to jot down some of the unique underlying characteristics of your student in the relevant boxes and reference the appropriate Automatic Door Opener QuickTip Sheets in proactively planning your classroom design and instruction, based on the individual profile of the particular student you are welcoming to your class. For instance, perhaps the student does not have a great deal of difficulty with executive function but struggles more with social issues and mindblindness. If so, you may wish to focus first on the Automatic Door Opener QuickTip Sheets that support those characteristics.

Any way that you choose to use the Planning Guide, please remember that the Automatic Door Opener QuickTip Sheets are meant to be used proactively and on a class-wide basis and should not be viewed as a band-aid approach to addressing severe or acute individual issues. The Push to Open approach to classroom and instructional design does not preclude or eliminate the need to plan individual, intensive, and specialized supports for students with ASD and will not replace or reduce the importance of a comprehensive IEP for any student.

In the introduction of this book, we discussed the experience we all have had of approaching a place we need to enter but having our arms too full to open the door. The automatic door opener does not eliminate all the packages you are holding. It does not perform the tasks you need to accomplish in the building once you are there. It does not even give you a strategy for trying to gain entry to another building that is not accessible. However, when used proactively, the Push to Open approach helps hold open the doors for all of your students to participate, learn, grow, and meet their potential in your classroom. And isn't that what we want for ALL of our students?

References

American Psychiatric Association. (2013). *Diagnostic and statistical manual of mental disorders* (5th ed.). Arlington, VA: Author.

Ashburner, J., Ziviani, J., & Rodger, S. (2008). Sensory processing and classroom emotional, behavioral, and educational outcomes in children with autism spectrum disorder. *American Journal of Occupational Therapy, 62,* 564-573.

Aspy, R., & Grossman, B. (2008). *The ziggurat model. A framework for designing comprehensive interventions for individuals with high functioning autism and Asperger syndrome.* Shawnee Mission, KS: AAPC Publishing.

Baker, J. (2003). *Social skills training for children and adolescents with Asperger syndrome and social communication problems.* Shawnee Mission, KS: AAPC Publishing.

Baker, J. (2008). *No more meltdowns. Positive strategies for managing and preventing out of control behavior.* Arlington, TX: Future Horizons, Inc.

Bayle, D. J, Henaff, M. A., & Krolak-Salmon, P. (2009). *Unconsciously perceived fear in peripheral vision alerts the limbic system.* Retrieved from http://www.plosone.org/article/info%3A-doi%2F10.1371%2Fjournal.pone.0008207

Bloom, B. J. (1956). *Taxonomy of educational objectives.* White Plains, NY: Longman.

Boyd, B., McDonough, S., & Bodfish, J. (2012). Evidence-based behavioral interventions for repetitive behaviors in autism. *Journal of Autism and Developmental Disorders, 42*(6), 1236-1248.

Bradley, R., Danielson, L., & Doolittle, J. (2005). Response to Intervention. *Journal of Learning Disabilities, 38*(6), 485-486.

Brown, C., & Stoffel, V. (2011). *Occupational therapy in mental health: A vision for participation.* Philadelphia, PA: F. A. Davis Company.

Cara, E., & MacRae, E. (2013). *Psychosocial occupational therapy: An evolving practice.* Clifton Park, NY: Delmar, Cengage Learning.

Cardon, T. (2007). *Initiations and interactions: Early intervention techniques for parents of children with autism spectrum disorders.* Shawnee Mission, KS: AAPC Publishing.

CAST. (2011). *Universal design for learning guidelines, version 2.0.* Wakefield, MA: Author.

CAST. (2014). *CAST through the years: One mission, many innovations.* Retrieved from http://www.cast.org/about/timeline/index.html

Centers for Disease Control and Prevention. (2014). *CDC estimates 1 in 68 children has been identified with autism spectrum disorder.* Retrieved from http://www.cdc.gov/media/releases/2014/p0327-autism-spectrum-disorder.html

Collucci, A. Z. (2011). *Big picture thinking: Using central coherence theory to support social skills.* Shawnee Mission, KS: AAPC Publishing.

"Core Principles of PBIS." (2014). Retrieved from http://www.pbis.org/school/primary-level

Coucouvanis, J. (2005). *Super skills: A social skills group program for children with Asperger syndrome, high functioning autism and related challenges.* Shawnee Mission, KS: AAPC Publishing.

Coyne, P., & Rood, K. (2011). *Executive function and organization for youth with autism spectrum disorder.* Retrieved from http://crporegon.org/system/files/documents/AUT_Unit3.3%20Organization.pdf

Culp, S. (2011). *A buffet of sensory interventions: Solutions for middle and high school students with autism spectrum disorders.* Shawnee Mission, KS: AAPC Publishing.

Davis, K., & Duble, M. (n.d.). *Sensory integration: Tips to consider.* Retrieved from http://www.iidc.indiana.edu/?pageId=471

Doman, R. J. (2006). *The selective use of TV and videos for advancing the development of special needs, typical and accelerated preschool children.* Retrieved from http://nacd.org/journal/television

Dunn Buron, K., & Curtis, M. (2013). *The incredible 5-point scale* (2nd ed.). Shawnee Mission, KS: AAPC Publishing.

Dunn Buron, K., & Wolfberg, P. (2014). *Learners on the autism spectrum: Preparing highly qualified educators* (2nd ed.). Shawnee Mission, KS: Autism Asperger Publishing Company.

Dunn, W. (2007). Supporting children to participate successfully in everyday life by using sensory processing knowledge. *Infants and Young Children 20*(2), 84-101.

Endow, J. (2009). *Outsmarting explosive behavior: A visual system of support and intervention for individuals with autism spectrum disorders.* Shawnee Mission, KS: Autism Asperger Publishing Company.

Endow, J. (2011). *Practical solutions for stabilizing students with classic autism to be ready to learn: Getting to go!* Shawnee Mission, KS: Autism Asperger Publishing Company.

Evidence-Based Practice Briefs. (2014). Retrieved from http://autismpdc.fpg.unc.edu/content/briefs

Flores, M. M., Nelson, C., Hinton, V., Franklin, T. M., Strozier, S. D., Terry, L., & Franklin, S. (2013). Teaching reading comprehension and language skills to students with autism spectrum disorders and developmental disabilities using direct instruction. *Education and Training in Autism and Developmental Disabilities, 48*(1), 41-48.

Freschi, D. (2006, January/February). Plan today for generalizations tomorrow. *Autism Asperger's Digest.* Retrieved from http://autismdigest.com/plan-today-for-generalizations-tomorrow/

Gardner, H. (1983). *Frames of mind: The theory of multiple intelligences.* New York, NY: Basic Books.

Gray, C. (2010). *The new social story book.* Arlington, TX: Future Horizons.

Grossman, R. B., & Tager-Flusberg, H. (2012). Quality matters! Differences between expressive and receptive communication skills in adolescents with ASD. *Research in Autism Spectrum Disorders, 6*(3), 1150-1155.

Hall, T. E., Meyer, A., & Rose, D. H. (2012). *Universal design for learning in the classroom. Practical applications.* New York, NY: The Guilford Press.

Howlin, P., Baron-Cohen, S., & Hadwin, J. (1999). *Teaching children with autism to mind-read: A practical guide.* New York, NY: John Wiley and Sons.

Hume, K. (2013). *Visual supports (VS) fact sheet.* Chapel Hill: The University of North Carolina, Frank Porter Graham Child Development Institute, The National Professional Development Center on Autism Spectrum Disorders.

Hunter, M. (1976). Teacher competency: Problem, theory and practice. *Theory into Practice, 15*(2), 161-171.

Jenson, E. (2005). *Teaching with the brain in mind.* Alexandria, VA: Association for Supervision and Curriculum Development.

Kabot, S., & Reeve, C. (2010). *Setting up classroom spaces that support students with autism spectrum disorders.* Shawnee Mission, KS: AAPC Publishing.

Kerstein, L. (2008). *My sensory book: Working together to explore sensory issues and the big feelings they cause: A workbook for parents, professionals, and children.* Shawnee Mission, KS: AAPC Publishing.

Kinnealey, M., Pfeiffer, B., Miller, J., Roan, C., Shoener, R., & Ellner, M. L. (2012). Effect of classroom modification on attention and engagement of students with autism or dyspraxia. *American Journal of Occupational Therapy, 66,* 511-519.

Kluth, P. (2003). *You're going to love this kid.* Baltimore, MD: Paul H. Brookes Publishing Co.

Kluth, P., & Chandler-Olcott, K. (2008). *A land we can share.* Baltimore, MD: Paul H. Brookes Publishing Co.

Kluth, P., & Schwartz, P. (2008). *Just give him the whale.* Baltimore, MD: Paul H. Brookes Publishing Co.

Kranowitz, C. (1998). *The out of sync child: recognizing and coping with sensory integration dysfunction.* New York, NY: The Berkley Publishing Group.

Krusemark, E., Novak, R., Gitelman, D., & Li, W. (2013). When the sense of smell meets emotion: Anxiety-state-dependent olfactory processing and neural circuitry adaptation. *The Journal of Neuroscience, 33*(9), 15324-15332.

Kwayke, L. D., Foss-Feig, J. H., Cascio, C. J., Stone, W. L., & Wallace, M. T. (2011). Altered auditory and multisensory temporal processing in autism spectrum disorders. *Frontiers in Integrative Neuroscience.* doi:10.3389/fnint.2010.00129

Lavoie, R. (2007). *The motivation breakthrough: 6 secrets to turning on the tuned-out child.* New York, NY: Touchstone A Division of Simon & Schuster, Inc.

Leekam, S. R., Nieto, C., Libby, S., & Wing, L. (2007). Describing the sensory abnormalities of children and adults with autism. *Journal of Autism and Developmental Disorders, 37,* 894-910.

Lewis, R., & Doorlag, D. (2003). *Teaching special students in general education classrooms,* Upper Saddle River, NJ: Merrill Prentice Hall.

McMains, S., & Kastner, S. (2011). Interactions of top-down and bottom-up mechanisms in human visual cortex. *Journal of Neuroscience, 31*(2), 587-597.

Meadan, H., Ostrosky, M. M., Triplett, B., Michna, A., & Fettig, A. (2011). Using visual supports with young children with autism spectrum disorder. *Teaching Exceptional Children, 43*(6), 28-35.

Menasco, H. (2006). *The way to a: Empowering children with autism spectrum and other neurological disorders to monitor and replace aggressive and tantrum behavior.* Shawnee Mission, KS: AAPC Publishing.

Moyes, R. (2002). *Addressing the challenging behavior of children with high functioning autism/Asperger syndrome in the classroom: A guide for teachers and parents.* Philadelphia, PA: Jessica Kingsley Publishers.

Myles, B., Adreon, D., & Gitlitz, D. (2006). *Simple strategies that work! Helpful hints for all educators of students with Asperger Syndrome, high functioning autism, and related disabilities.* Shawnee Mission, KS: AAPC Publishing.

Myles, B. S., Hagiwara, T., Dunn, W., Rinner, L., & Reese, M. (2004). Sensory issues in children with Asperger Syndrome and autism. *Education and Training in Developmental Disabilities, 39*(4), 283-290.

Myles, B. S., Mahler, K., & Robbins, L. (2014). *Sensory issues and high-functioning autism spectrum and related disorders – Practical solutions for making sense of the world* (2nd ed.). Shawnee Mission, KS: AAPC Publishing.

Myles, B. S., Trautman, M. L., & Schelvan, R. (2013). *The hidden curriculum for understanding unstated rules in social situations for adolescents and young adults.* Shawnee Mission, KS: AAPC Publishing.

National Research Council. (2001). *Educating children with autism.* Washington, DC: National Academy Press.

Ochs, E., Kremer-Sadlik, T., Solomon, O., & Gainer Sirota, K. (2001). *Inclusion as social practice: Views of children with autism.* Retrieved from http://www.ssc.ucla.edu/anthro/faculty/ochs/articles/Inclusion_As_Social_Practice.pdf

O'Connor, A. (2012, September 3). *School bullies prey on children with autism.* Retrieved from http://well.blogs.nytimes.com/2012/09/03/school-bullies-prey-on-children-with-autism/?_php=true&_type=blogs&_r=0

Ogle, D. (1986). K-W-L: A teaching model that develops active reading of expository test. *Reading Teacher, 39*, 564-570.

Rafferty, L. (2010). Step-by-step: Teaching students to self-monitor. *Teaching Exceptional Children, 43*(2), 50-58.

Rapp, W. (2014). *Universal design for learning in action.* Baltimore, MD: Paul Brookes Publishing Co.

Reeve, C., & Kabot, S. (2012). *Building independence: How to create and use structured work systems.* Shawnee Mission, KS: AAPC Publishing.

Regier, N. (2012). *Focus on student learning – Instructional strategies series.* Weyburn, Sask., Canada: Regier Educational Resources.

Rosenshine, B. (2012, Spring). Principles of instruction. Research-based strategies that every teacher should know. *American Educator, 12-39.*

Rudy, L. J. (2014). *Repetitive behaviors in autism.* Retrieved from http://autism.about.com/od/whatisautism/a/perseveration.htm

Salend, S. (2011). *Creating inclusive classrooms: Effective and reflective practices.* Upper Saddle River, NJ: Pearson Education, Inc.

Schunk, D. H. (1983). Progress self-monitoring: Effects on children's self-efficacy and achievement. *Journal of Experimental Education, 51,* 89-93.

Schwartz, P., & Kluth, P. (2007). *You're welcome: 30 innovative ideas for the inclusive classroom.* Portsmouth, NH: Heinemann.

Snyder, T. D., & Dillow, S. A. (2013). *Digest of education statistics 2012 (NCES 2014-015).* Washington, DC: U.S. Department of Education, National Center for Education Statistics, Institute of Education Sciences.

Sousa, D., & Tomlinson, C. A. (2011). *Differentiation and the brain.* Bloomington, IN: Solution Tree Press.

Stewart, R. (n.d.). *Motivating students who have autism spectrum disorders.* Retrieved from http://www.iidc.indiana.edu/?pageId=430

Stoke, S. (n.d.). *Developing expressive communication skills for non-verbal children with autism.* Retrieved from http://www.specialed.us/autism/nonverbal/non11.htm

Tomlinson, C. (1999). *The differentiated classroom: Responding to the needs of all learners.* Alexandria, VA: Association for Supervision and Curriculum Development.

Tomlinson, C. (2001a). *How to differentiate instruction in mixed-ability classrooms.* Alexandria, VA: Association for Supervision and Curriculum Development.

Tomlinson, C. (2001b). *At work in the differentiated classroom.* Alexandria, VA: Association for Supervision and Curriculum Development.

UDL Guidelines 2.0. (2011). Retrieved from http://www.udlcenter.org/aboutudl/udlguidelines

What is universal design for learning? (n.d.). Retrieved from http://cast.org/udl/index.html

Wilczynski, S. M., & Pollack, E. G. (Eds.). (2009). *Evidence-based practice and autism in the schools: A guide to providing appropriate interventions to students with autism spectrum disorders.* Randolph, MA: National Autism Center.

Winebrenner, S. (1992). *Teaching gifted kids in the regular classroom.* Minneapolis, MN: Free Spirit.

Winebrenner, S. (1996). *Teaching kids with learning difficulties in the regular classroom.* Minneapolis, MN: Free Spirit.

Winner, M. (2002). *Thinking about you, thinking about me.* San Jose, CA: Michelle Garcia Winner Publishing.

Appendix

Automatic Door Openers:
Push to Open QuickTip Sheets

REDUCING AUDITORY CLUTTER

- Teach students the "inside voice" concept. Teach students to be aware of how far away their voice can be heard. You can use 6 inch, 12 inch, 24 inch, and 36 inch spacers and practice volume to see how soft voice volume would have to be to be heard only 6 inches away, 12 inches away, etc. This gives students a common vocabulary so that you can use a direction such as, "You may work in partners, but please use a 6 inch voice," and the students will know what the expected volume is.

- Close classroom door to reduce hallway noise.

- Play low-volume, calming music during independent work to mask unpredictable noise.

- Use a quiet tone of voice when instructing.

- Use a classroom amplification system to "pop" teacher voice over ambient classroom noise without having to change teacher volume, pitch, or tone. Many newer schools are equipped with built-in speaker systems to which are connected microphones that the teacher wears on a lanyard around her neck or clipped to her clothing. Older classrooms can be retrofitted with these systems as well.

- Use a stoplight system to indicate the noise level allowed. When the red light is on, the only person talking should be the teacher. Yellow means that the students may talk within the learning activity, such as a group project. The green light indicates indoor recess or social time.

- Use thumbs up or thumbs down to indicate to students whether they need to speak up or quiet down.

- Post schedules and duties for adults in the room to eliminate need for communicating duties verbally.

- Reduce off-topic conversation between adults.

- Develop and systematically teach simple visual cues to replace frequently used phrases, reminders, directions, and redirections.

- Choose an attention-getting visual cue to signal class-wide silence and attention (lights off or light blinking, etc.), rather than yelling over noise and other distractions.

REDUCING VISUAL CLUTTER

- Store materials in closed cupboards, closets, or solid-colored bins when not in use.

- Cover open bookshelves, cupboards, and cubbies with solid, dark-colored curtains or sheeting.

- Use single-colored paper as backgrounds on bulletin boards.

- Avoid bright and busy patterns for curtains, bulletin board backings, borders, rugs, etc.

- Make instructional visual supports on charts or posters that "come and go" as needed to prevent accumulation of too many visuals throughout the year. For example, one teacher taped a "hands to yourself" picture on a student's desk as a reminder not to touch his neighboring students or their possessions. However, since it was there all the time, the student became accustomed to it and didn't notice it after a while. As an alternative, the teacher kept the reminder card in her pocket and showed it to the student only when she noticed him beginning to touch others. This brought it to his attention only when needed.

- Preserve some blank wall space.

- Delineate one area or bulletin board for student work.

- Avoid hanging artwork or seasonal décor from the ceiling. The movement of these items as people walk through can be distracting to students who have visual sensitivity. Artwork is better hung on a static display, such as a bulletin board.

- Use natural light when possible as an alternative to fluorescent light.

- Avoid use of window clings to allow for calming visual access to the outdoors.

- Place necessary visual supports, such as ABC strips, on student desks rather than on far-point display.

CREATING CALMING SENSORY INPUT

- Incorporate regular movement breaks within and between activities.

- Allow students to use water bottles throughout the day.

- Delineate a "quiet corner" with a bean bag, headphones, reduced lighting, and barriers to reduce visual input. The quiet corner could also include a rocking chair and some preferred books or music.

- Provide stress balls or other fidgets.

- Do 5-10 minutes of simple stretching or movement activities, such as touch toes, jogging in place, chair pushes, and wall push-ups.

- Give directions using slow, soft voice cadence.

- Exercise with resistance bands. Consult with your occupational therapist for specific exercises.

- Use modeling clay activities/play dough for pinching, squeezing, fidgeting.

- Have students do chair push-ups between activities.

- Have students do wall pushes while waiting in the hall.

- Have students push hands together while waiting to be called on.

- Have students stack/un-stack classroom chairs, move desks/heavy bins for various activities.

- If providing snacks, emphasize chewy snacks.

CREATING CLEAR VISUAL AND PHYSICAL BOUNDARIES

- Arrange furniture and room furnishings to delineate or "define" different areas of the room for specific purposes. For example, a reading area bordered by bookshelves, a circle time area delineated by a rug with numbered spaces for students to sit on, a computer station at the back of the room along a wall, and various learning stations indicated by study carrels.

- Use rugs, colored tape, carpet squares, moveable shelving units, dividers, or curtains to create boundary lines between floor spaces.

- Create smaller learning areas rather that one large open area.

- Use colored tape, placemats, name tags, and color-coded bins on desks and tables to help students recognize the boundaries of their own space.

- Provide clearly defined areas for independent work, one-on-one, and small-group and large-group instruction.

- Post specific behavioral expectations for a given area within the area in a place that students see immediately upon entrance. For instance, post a sign near the entrance to the reading corner as follows: "Welcome to the Reading Corner! Only three readers are allowed here at one time. Choose a book, choose a seat, and read quietly so that everyone can enjoy some quiet reading time together!" Hang three "reading passes" on hooks by the entrance. If students don't find any reading passes hanging there, it means that the reading corner is full and there are no spots available.

- Use tri-fold presentation boards to close off areas such as the computer when not available for student use.

- Use study carrels or turn desk to face the wall between shelving to create boundaries to individual workspaces.

- Designate an adult area in the room for teacher desk, computer, phone, filing cabinets, etc., and make a clear boundary around it.

INCORPORATING DAILY OPPORTUNITIES FOR LEARNING SOCIAL SKILLS

- Choose a weekly social skill to work on as a class (example: taking turns in conversation), practice it as a group, and then issue tickets for students "caught" demonstrating that skill and enter them in a raffle.

- Begin each day with a conversation starter and partner or group discussion. (Example: What did you have for dinner last night? What pets do you have or want? How do you like the book we are reading in language arts?)

- During indoor recess, structure and supervise activities/games that support specific social skills such as "Simon Says" (listening and following a direction), "Mother, May I?" (asking and awaiting permission), and charades (watching and interpreting nonverbals).

- Draw names of 2-3 students to eat lunch with the teacher occasionally.

- Teach the "hidden curriculum" or the unwritten rules that may have gone unnoticed or misunderstood by some students. Specific strategies may be found in the Recommended Resources section.

TEACHING AND INCORPORATING SELF-MANAGEMENT SKILLS

- Have an anchor activity of either journal writing or partner discussion first thing in the morning for each student to note their emotional state and then what they will need to do that day to help them self-manage. For students who have more limited written expression skills, this may be as simple as having them circle a happy face, sad face, angry face, etc., to indicate their feelings as they begin the day.

- Have bins of stress balls and fidgets available for use. Teach behavioral expectations (no throwing, no placing in mouth, etc.) from the beginning of the year.

- Provide a home base, quiet corner, or "vacation" area where students can go when they need a short break. Teach and reinforce behavioral expectations for accessing the home base. For instance, set up a system whereby the students have to give a "pass" or "break card" to one of the adults in the room to indicate the need for a break and get approval before going to the home base area. The student will also need to know what activities are allowed in the home base area.

- Practice deep breathing with the whole class during transition times, after recess, before tests, after fire drills, etc. Follow the "1:2" inhale:exhale ratio (example: count to 3 as you breathe in, count to 6 as you breathe out).

- Hang a "What I Can Do During Down Time" poster. Example: doing jigsaw puzzles, reading silently, journal writing, drawing, reading/looking at magazines, play dough.

REDUCING UNNECESSARY MOVEMENT

- Plan the classroom layout to include direct and obvious pathways to and from important locations, such as the teacher desk, the computer station, the small-group instruction area, the tissues, the pencil sharpener, and homework turn-in area.

- Teach and practice expectations about student movement within the room, such as taking the most direct route to and from your destination.

- Give students a flag or table tent to put up to indicate a need for assistance and have the adult move to students rather than having the students line up at the teacher desk to wait.

- Institute a "parking lot" in one corner of the room and provide sticky notes for students to post questions that "can wait" (such as "What are we having for lunch?" "When is the field trip?" etc.).

- Teach, practice, and enforce "personal space" respect among students. For example, provide boundaries such as paper footprints on the floor where students stand in line, carpet squares to sit on for floor activities, and painter's tape boundaries on the floor around work areas, or periodically practice determining the appropriate space to stand from someone using hoola hoops.

- Write task-specific directions, examples, and information on a Smartboard (www.smarttech.com) for student reference to prevent unnecessary student trips to ask questions.

PROVIDING FREQUENT MOVEMENT BREAKS

- Have students do a short series of movements at natural transition points – between subjects, activities or location changes (example:10 touch toes, 10 chair or desk push-ups, 30 seconds of jogging in place, head-shoulder-knees and toes, etc.).

- Lead a short series of yoga poses before lunch. Choose positions that don't require a great deal of space or difficult motor planning. Suitable positions include warrior, downward dog, mountain, forward fold. Specific resources for yoga routines are listed in the Recommended Resources section.

- Post laminated handprints in the hallway where students can do wall push-ups while they wait in restroom or water fountain line.

- With younger children, have the students "animal walk" from location to location (bear walk, elephant walk, bunny hop, etc.).

- Incorporate kinesthetic activities into lessons (skits, role-play, field trips, nature walks, etc.).

PROVIDING VISUAL SUPPORTS

- Post no more than five classroom rules with simple illustrations in a prominent location in the room and leave them in the same location all year. For example, 1) Follow the teacher's directions. 2) Be kind to other students. 3) Take care of our classroom. 4) Speak in a quiet voice. 5) Ask an adult before leaving the room.

- Make sure the rules are appropriate for the age and developmental level of the students. The key is to keep them simple and easy to remember. Many teachers create an acronym from their rules to make them even easier to remember. I saw a "STAR" rule chart used in a third-grade classroom: 1) Stay focused on the lesson. 2) Try your best on all assignments. 3) Act safely and kindly. 4) Respect your fellow students.

- Post the daily classroom schedule in a prominent and consistent location.

- Check off, erase, or otherwise indicate items that are completed on the classroom schedule periodically through the day or allow a student to do so.

- Provide individual schedules for students who need a more detailed schedule to mark the passage of time and to prime for future activities.

- Provide mini-schedules for learning centers, individual work, or large-group instructional periods.

- Use cue cards (simple pictures that you can keep on a key ring or lanyard) to replace or support frequently used phrases ("good job," "quiet please," etc.).

- Use consistent color coding to indicate subjects, locations, materials, etc.

Boardmaker®; www.mayer-johnson.com

- Provide written or pictorial directions to accompany verbal directions.

- Use consistent gestures (such as thumbs up, thumbs down, finger to lips, etc.) to accompany or replace verbal feedback.

Boardmaker®; www.mayer-johnson.com

COMMUNICATING IN A CRISIS

- Reduce or eliminate verbal interaction.

- Give the student physical space.

- If necessary, approach the student visibly from the front or the side, never from behind.

- Avoid light or unexpected touch, such as a tap on the shoulder.

- Use visual cues or gestures.

- When speaking, use a calm, quiet voice.

- Allow the student time to de-escalate before trying to process what happened.

- Phrase any directives in short, positive statements of what to do, instead of what *not* to do.

- Refrain from participating in arguments or verbal power struggles.

CREATING PURPOSEFUL MOVEMENT BREAKS

- Use natural transition points between lessons, locations, or activities to lead a short movement break, such as 10 touch toes or 10 chair push-ups.

- Incorporate movement into academic activities through role-play, skits, nature walks, etc.

- As you prepare the class to line up, have the students form a line and "cha-cha" once around the room to the door. Do "the wave" in celebration of finishing a book, a test, or a tough math lesson, just like fans do at an athletic event.

- Periodically throughout the day, between activities, take a slip of paper from a jar and read the direction: "Do five touch toes," "Flap your arms like a chicken," or "Run in place."

- Incorporate Brain Gym® activities into the classroom schedule (http://www.braingym.org/).

- Incorporate a 10- to 15-minute yoga session at a certain point in the day (avoid yoga for at least 90 minutes after a meal).

- Teach and lead calming breathing techniques (hands on the belly, count 3 on the inhale, count 6 on the exhale) at points in the day after recess or other high-energy activities, or prior to high-stress situations like tests.

CREATING A COMFORTABLE PHYSICAL CLIMATE

- Use natural or incandescent light if possible rather than fluorescent light.

- Keep the room temperature moderate, allowing students to use appropriate layers of clothing to adjust for personal comfort.

- Avoid scented candles, air fresheners, strongly scented perfumes, lotions, hairsprays, etc.

- Allow personal space of at least hula hoop size for all students, if possible, but especially for students with tactile sensitivity.

- Have an occupational therapist assess seat and desk sizes to ensure appropriate height and depth for age and size of students.

- Provide a "quiet corner" for students to take a break from activities or sensory input.

PROVIDING SOCIAL-EMOTIONAL SUPPORT

- Teach, practice, model, and reinforce kindness, respect, and tolerance of others every single minute of every single day.

- Begin the school year with one or two student orientation days (see Auto Door Opener for specific ideas) to get to know students and help them get to know each other.

- Dedicate a wall space or bulletin board for recognition of Random Acts of Kindness.

- Create a class Yellow Pages that lists the students by what special talents they have to help others ("Proofreaders," "Artists," etc.).

- Never use sarcasm.

- Use teachable moments to model mediation and negotiation skills for students when a problem arises between peers.

- Model for students that it is O.K. to make mistakes or say they don't know something by doing so yourself on a regular basis.

- Offer opportunities to correct work, and give academic credit for improvement.

USING POSITIVE BEHAVIOR SUPPORTS

- Teach behavioral expectations using the same teaching model that you would for any academic skill: Objectives, Standards, Set, Teaching, Guided Practice, Closure, Independent Practice.

- Provide meaningful incentives, recognizing that some students have unique interests and may not be motivated by traditional incentives like extra recess or a popcorn party but require individualized supports.

- Provide meaningful consequences, recognizing that some students are not concerned about or even feel rewarded by traditional consequences like "missing recess" or "going to the principal" and, therefore, require individualized supports.

- Recognize triggers of undesired behavior and attempt to proactively solve the problem by removing the trigger (sensory overload, frustration, bullying).

Note. These ideas for assessing readiness and many more may be found in *Focus on Student Learning – Instructional Series* by Natalie Regier, MEd (2012).

ASSESSING READINESS

- Incorporate a wide variety of multi-modal methods to quickly pre-assess student knowledge:

    - KWL Charts: Students record what they know, what they want to know, and then what they learn (Ogle, 1986).

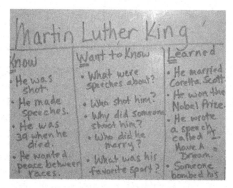

    - Graffiti Groups: Pairs, triads, or quads of students create graffiti-style posters of what they know about a topic.

    - "YES/NO" Cards: Students indicate understanding as the teacher asks a variety of questions on the topic to be studied next. For instance, while doing a science experiment, give each student an index card taped to a popsicle stick. On one side is written "Yes" and the other side, "No." As the teacher asks questions during the experiment, such as  "Do you think the solution will change color?," the students put up their card with either a "Yes" or a "No." This allows the teacher to quickly assess student understanding. If many students have the wrong answer, she can decide to review information or ask additional questions before moving on.

- Think/Pair/Share: Students formulate their own opinions and then discuss in pairs.

- Four Corners: The four corners of the room are labeled "Strongly Agree," "Agree," "Disagree," "Strongly Disagree." To assess higher-level thinking skills like prediction and evaluation, the teacher reads statements about the lesson's topic, and the students move to the corner that best describes their opinion about it.

- Card Sort: Students match cards with questions to cards with answers (examples: word cards matched with their definition cards, or math problems matched with their corresponding answer cards). The card sets may be sorted by an individual or used in a variety of games (e.g., *Concentration*) with groups of students.

- Carrousel: Chart paper labeled with key vocabulary words is placed around the room. Students move from poster to poster, adding either words or illustrations to depict each word or concept.

INCORPORATING STUDENTS' SPECIAL INTERESTS AND ACTIVITIES

- Provide many cross-curricular opportunities for students to choose topics for writing, reading, or investigating.

- Link behavior incentives to special interests (time on the computer to study an interest, engaging in a preferred activity or hobby, etc.).

- Provide opportunities for students to engage in conversation on topics of special interest. An exceptional kindergarten teacher created a special time each morning called "Buzz Time" when students paired up with a different buddy each day and were given a topic to discuss such as "What is your favorite food?" or "If you could have any animal for a pet, what would it be?" This gave the students the opportunity to develop basic social skills like taking turns, asking questions, and showing interest in others while also having time to talk about their own interests and preferences.

- Incorporate special interest subjects into academic tasks (topics for reports, story problems in math, choice of manipulative, scientific inquiry, etc.).

- Set up webquests or virtual field trips as a learning center, where you can include topics of special interest to many students throughout the year. For examples of webquests, go to www.webquest.org.

- Allow independent reading/study/research/computer work as an anchor activity when students have completed other assignments.

- Schedule time for students to speak, present, or show a film to the class on a topic of special interest or talent.

CONDUCTING STUDENT ORIENTATION

- Use the first few days of school to conduct student orientation, including introduction to the classroom rules, learning locations in the room and school, and practicing daily routines.

- Set up learning stations where students can take self-assessments such as learning style assessments, multiple intelligence surveys, interest inventories, etc. Even young students can complete a survey showing pictures of different activities (drawing, playing outside, looking at books, talking to friends, etc.) with a happy face and an unhappy face by each. Students color either the happy or the unhappy face to show whether they like or do not like a given activity. Make a graph on the board showing how many like to read, how many like to play outside, etc. This not only helps students know that there are others who share their interest but also introduces the concept of graphic representation of data, which is part of the Common Core mathematics content standards.

- Teach, model, and practice classroom procedures, rules, and routines.

- Teach, model, and practice acceptable voice volume, movement among locations, and handling of materials.

- Compile class "Yellow Pages" directory according to student talents and interests so that students can look up peers when needing assistance.

- Let students make personalized name tags or desk placards to help them get to know one another's names and interests.

- Conduct a variety of ice-breakers to help students get comfortable with one another. Example, at the beginning of a new year, bring in a small brown bag filled with items that represent your own interests or things that are important to you (pictures of your family kids, hobbies, trips, etc.). Then give each student a brown bag to bring in items about themselves to share. This gives students an opportunity to show others their interests and talents, what makes them unique, and also what they might have in common with others in the class.

SUPPORTING CENTRAL COHERENCE

- Use advance organizers for students to preview the concepts to be covered in a unit and to see how concepts relate to each other.

- Provide skeleton outlines for students to take notes during class.

- Provide PowerPoint handouts for students to follow lectures and take notes.

- Prior to students working independently, model an example showing each step of a task.

- Use a variety of cooperative grouping options for students to support one another in task completion. Some activities are best done in pairs while for others it is better to assign students to specific assigned roles. For instance, assigned to do a report on one of the 50 states, a cooperative group offers the chance for all the students in a group to study the same materials but play different roles in the finished learning product. An excellent reader may do the bulk of the reading aloud in a group where other students benefit from hearing the information. A student who struggles with written expression but is a fantastic artist may contribute to a group project by illustrating concepts that another student is writing about and a third student is presenting verbally to the class.

- Provide both far-point and near-point written or illustrated step-by-step directions for tasks.

- Teach students a process for self-monitoring and self-checking the quality of their work. Provide a "conference time" with you for students to review their "sloppy copy" of written work. At that time, go through a checklist with them, to guide them in checking for specific criteria that they will be graded on. (For instance, the checklist may ask them to check for: Capitals at the beginning of each sentence, a period or question mark at the end of each sentence, a topic sentence, and at least three Details.) Model the process for them so that eventually they become independent in using the checklist to check their work before they turn it in.

- Use "peer buddies" to help students check each other's work, assist one another, and provide modeling.

SUPPORTING TRANSFER
AND GENERALIZATION

- Use strategy sheets, cue cards, and scripts to help students remember what to do in various situations (e.g. "What to say if you don't agree with someone?").

- Ensure that all teachers working with the same group of students have consistent behavioral expectations and reinforcement systems.

- Teach, model, and practice the "look fors" in situations (example: "If all the other students are seated, I should sit down, too.").

- Teach students to ask teachers for feedback and reinforcement if they are not certain whether they are doing the right thing.

- Provide role-playing opportunities to practice skills in a variety of contexts.

- Videotape examples and non-examples to let the class problem solve as a group.

- Prime students for expectations in new locations, experiences, and activities.

- Provide opportunities to practice skills in a variety of settings, across subjects, and in different locations.

PROVIDING OPTIONS FOR PERCEPTION

- Use technology to customize font style and size, and contrast of print to background to make materials easily modifiable for different students. For instance, if a worksheet is taken straight from the math workbook, the amount of information on the page may be overwhelming for some students. Creating a worksheet on the computer enables you to enlarge the font, include fewer problems on a page, and put borders around each problem to make it easier and less overwhelming for the student to complete.

- Provide software that enables students to hear text being read aloud to them through text-to-speech options (example: Write Out Loud, www. donjohnston.com; Kurzweil 3000, www.kurzweiledu.com).

- Provide a word processing option for written expression to allow for word prediction, text to speech "read back," and grammar and spell check.

- Provide the option of the student dictating lengthy written assignments rather than writing/typing them. This may be done through the speech recognition function on most word processing programs, through the microphone of a tablet, or a computer application such as Dragon Dictate (www.nuance.com).

- Provide personal or classwide amplification systems to "pop" the teacher's voice above the ambient noise in the classroom.

- Use a Smartboard (www.smarttech.com) to allow for large, easily seen, interactive visual support during instruction.

- Use document cameras to provide modeling using actual materials on overhead screen. For instance, when going over a math worksheet, place the counting blocks or cubes onto the document camera's surface so that the students can see a projection of you moving the items into groups as you demonstrate the problem-solving process.

- Provide visual symbols that equate with verbal or auditory cues (such as a thumbs up or happy face for "good job").

- Use graphics, illustrations, and videos to illustrate or demonstrate key concepts.

PROVIDING CLARIFICATION OF SYMBOLS, EXPRESSIONS, AND LANGUAGE

- Pre-assess and pre-teach new vocabulary prior to each unit.

- Explicitly teach any new symbols that will be used in a lesson.

- Teach, model, and practice the use of context clues to figure out the meaning of unknown words.

- Teach, model, and practice structural analysis to assist students in the deconstruction of words to look for smaller known words, prefixes, suffixes, etc.

- Explain double meanings, figurative expressions, clichés, sarcasm, idioms, hyperbole, etc., as they are encountered in books, articles, films, etc.

- Use advance/graphic organizers to teach concepts like sentence structure, paragraph formation, summaries, etc.

- Use color coding or highlighting to indicate types of words, key words, and concepts, etc.

- Provide keys to frequently used symbols and teach key words to remember in connection with symbols and their functions (example: "The phrase 'how many more' in a story problem usually means you need to use the minus sign, or subtraction.").

PROVIDING OPTIONS
FOR COMPREHENSION

- Use multimedia materials to capture student interest, such as video clips, movies, music, art, or print materials related to the topic of the lesson.

- Provide background experience prior to instruction by linking it to prior learning or student experiences.

- Use graphic organizers to help students make connections between concepts.

- Use examples and non-examples to illustrate concepts.

- Ask guiding questions to lead students through the act of problem solving. For example, when approaching a story problem in math, ask such questions as "Do you see any words that might tell us whether to add or subtract?" or when approaching an unknown word in a reading passage, ask, "What sound does it begin with?"

- Provide manipulatives and hands-on experimentation with concepts. For example, have students use blocks, popsicle sticks, or other counting objects to learn how to trade single units for units of 10 when teaching place value.

- Provide multisensory options for exploration of concepts (literature, journal writing, role-play or dramatic reenactment, musical creation, artwork).

- Keep a jar of question words at different levels of Bloom's taxonomy and draw some out periodically when asking questions to prompt you to ask questions that require higher-level thinking.

- Rephrase questions using different words to teach students flexibility with vocabulary (example: find the answer, determine the answer, deduce the answer).

PROVIDING OPTIONS FOR
PHYSICAL ACTION

- Arrange the furniture in your classroom with wide aisles to allow for ease of movement, including students who use adaptive equipment, such as standing frames, wheelchairs, walkers, etc.

- Provide a variety of positional options for work tasks (desks, tables, standing easels, standing frames with desks, lying on floor).

- Provide options for interacting with materials (hands, mouse, joystick, switch, keyboard, etc.).

- Provide options for responding (bell instead of raising hand, voice output device rather than speaking).

- Keep necessary materials within easy reach for all who may need to access them.

- Provide dictation apps for students with fine-motor limitations for lengthy written assignments. For example, most smartphones, tablets, and computers have a microphone that allows students to dictate written work.

- Provide collaborative group activities where students with physical limitations can still participate fully in development of the product. For example, a student who has limited fine-motor skills and is not able to do the handwriting or artwork required for a presentation could still provide verbal input into developing the final product or press a switch to activate the PowerPoint slideshow when presenting a report to the class.

PROVIDING OPTIONS FOR EXPRESSION AND COMMUNICATION

- Provide multi-media options for students to create projects that demonstrate knowledge (PowerPoint, video, music, artwork, models, animations, etc.).

- Teach, model, and practice the use of advance/graphic organizers as a prewriting tool to brainstorm, organize, and prioritize ideas.

- Allow the use of technology to support written expression with word prediction, speech-to-text apps, spelling and grammar check, etc.

- Provide various learning style options for student products (skits, time-lines, charts, graphs, musical numbers, posters, collages, PowerPoint, diorama, collections, etc.).

- Encourage and respond enthusiastically to the student's mode of communication (verbal communication, sign language, voice output devices, pictures).

PROVIDING OPTIONS FOR EXECUTIVE FUNCTION

- Provide student agendas for keeping track of important dates, assignments, upcoming tests, etc.

- Teach students about personal goal setting by having all students set goals and monitor their progress throughout a set time period.

- Provide students with charts and checklists to assist them in monitoring their progress.

- Teach, model, and practice strategies for prioritizing tasks. For example, teach a lesson prior to a multi-step project in which you lead the whole group in deciding the order in which to do the steps (researching the topic, writing an outline, drawing the pictures, writing the report, etc.).

- Post suggested activities that students can engage in between tasks (independent reading, write in journals, partner practice multiplication flashcards).

- Provide students with graphic organizers (skeleton outlines, PowerPoint handouts and/or other teacher-created note-taking templates).

- Provide students detailed rubrics to be used for evaluation of assigned work.

Problem-Solving Rubric

Name: _____

Steps to Success	Pts.	Your Points
Correct Solution	3	
Solution Labeled	1	
Question Underlined	1	
Pictures Match Solution Strategies	2	
Calculations Correct	2	
Organization and Neatness	1	
Total	10	

RECRUITING INTEREST

- Plan the "anticipatory set" of the lesson by starting the lesson with a highly interesting and engaging activity, question, video, or brainteaser to intrigue, engage, and motivate learners.

- Allow students to choose topics that interest them whenever possible.

- When content is non-negotiable, allow students options for showing their attainment of knowledge through various types of projects (skits, musical numbers, PowerPoints, posters, etc.).

- Use instructional examples that are relevant to the students' age, gender, culture, and interests.

- Differentiate instruction for student ability to ensure all students experience success.

- Provide a wide variety of groupings to allow students to maintain a high level of participation and options to demonstrate their strengths in different roles (e.g., self-selected partners, random groups by counting off by 3's, groups based on similar abilities, groups based on common interests).

- Provide consistency in structure, routine, classroom organization, and behavioral expectations.

- Prime students for changes to lessen anxiety.

- Provide copious amounts of genuine praise and encouragement.

- Support and encourage risk-taking, asking questions, and experimentation.

SUSTAINING EFFORT AND PERSISTENCE

- Teach, model, and practice individual and class-wide goal setting.

- Explain learning objectives and keep them visible in easy-to-understand "I Can Statements" (example: "I can solve multiple step problems." "I can write a persuasive essay.").

- Provide individual and/or group incentives for task completion (example: post a bulletin board with pictures of empty ice cream cones, with each student's name on them. Students get to add a scoop on their ice cream cone for every spelling test they pass. When the whole class reaches a goal number of scoops, have a class ice cream party).

- Consider using learning contracts.

- Encourage the use of "peer buddies" to support and monitor work completion and quality. Differentiate complexity and task requirements based on student readiness.

- Incorporate student interests and learning styles in tasks.

- Provide many different options for independent and collaborative work.

- Provide regular, informative feedback in many forms (verbal, written, visual example, etc.).

- Give positive feedback and incentives for persistence, improvement, corrections, and attitude.

My Contract
Name: _____ Date: _____
These are my goals: 1. _____ 2. _____ 3. _____
These are my consequences if I don't meet my goals: _____ _____ _____
These are my rewards/positive consequences if I meet my goals: _____ _____ _____
My contract will be reviewed on: _____
Signatures: _____ _____
Peace, Love and Learning

SUPPORTING SELF-REGULATION

- Model and reinforce effective problem-solving on an individual and class-wide level.

- Encourage and model self-reflection and analysis of social situations. (Resources for specific strategies are listed in the Recommended Resources section.)

- Consider using a teaching method/curriculum for identifying emotions, expressing them, and responding to them in appropriate ways. (Resources for teaching emotional self-management are listed in the Recommended Resources section.)

- Use peers to model and reinforce appropriate interactions, responses, and reactions.

- Provide options for self-regulation through planned breaks (example: work with the occupational therapist to develop scheduled activities throughout the student's day).

- Teach appropriate and acceptable options for handling emotional escalation (example: teach students to ask for a break or ask permission to get a drink when getting frustrated).

- Teach and reinforce students' methods for monitoring their self-management (example: teach student to keep a chart where they give themselves a star for every class in which they followed directions without arguing).

- Provide individual and class-wide incentives for making good choices in communication and behavior (example: put marbles in a jar when students follow class expectations and have a class party when the jar is filled).

Recommended Resources

While the following list is by no means exhaustive, it represents materials, tools, and resources that I find myself returning to and recommending time and again when consulting with educational teams.

Resources for Teaching and Supporting Self-Management

The Incredible 5-Point Scale: The Significantly Improved and Expanded Second Edition; Assisting Students in Understanding Social Interactions and Controlling Their Emotional Responses, Kari Dunn Buron and Mitzi Curtis

This valuable resource provides a simple, adaptable color-coded 5-point scale to help students understand and monitor their emotions and feelings and choose the best possible responses to common occurrences that may cause them stress. The book guides teachers in identifying situations where students' emotional responses are leading to unexpected or troublesome reactions and provides guided student activities to create a 5-point scale identifying the triggering problem or event and suggesting alternative, positive responses at each level of the scale.

(Shawnee Mission, KS: AAPC Publishing, 2012)

The Way to A: Empowering Children With Autism Spectrum and Other Neurological Disorders to Monitor and Replace Aggression and Tantrum Behavior, Hunter Manasco

This simple tool provides a color-coded graphic organizer to help students proactively consider their behavioral options and the likely consequences, through an "A and B" flowchart. The program empowers students and reveals their incentives to make behavioral choices that will result in better outcomes for them. The laminated "write and wipe" format of the book allows it to be used over and over with the same student or various students.

(Shawnee Mission, KS: AAPC Publishing, 2006)

Outsmarting Explosive Behavior: A Visual System of Support and Intervention for Individuals With Autism Spectrum Disorders, Judy Endow

This system of visual supports utilizes the analogy of a runaway train to help students understand how their emotional state can escalate and subsequently develop a plan of strategies for stopping the chain reaction that often leads to meltdown. The tool provides everything the teacher needs with write-on train-themed manipulatives and a four-pocket foldout that allows students to interact with the tool and customize it for their unique triggers and reactions.

(Shawnee Mission, KS: AAPC Publishing, 2009)

Resources for Teaching Social Understanding and Social Interaction Skills

The Hidden Curriculum for Understanding Unstated Rules in Social Situations for Adolescents and Young Adults, Brenda Smith Myles, Melissa L. Trautman, and Rhonda L. Schelvan

This book is a "one stop shop" for ideas on how to teach the many complex aspects of social interactions to students who struggle with the "unwritten rules" of social interaction. The authors give overviews of strategies that are particularly useful for adolescent students and young adults, and provide many visual supports and templates for helping students navigate the challenges of a variety of social situations.

(Shawnee Mission, KS: AAPC Publishing, 2013)

Thinking About You, Thinking About Me, 2nd Edition, Michelle Garcia Winner

This is a key resource in understanding and addressing the needs of students who have difficulty with taking the perspective of others (also known as theory of mind). The book includes assessment tools as well as lesson planning activities, templates for instruction, and student handouts for a variety of age levels.

(New York, NY: Jessica Kingsley Publishers, 2002)

Social Skills Training for Children and Adolescents With Asperger Syndrome and Social Communication Problems, Jed Baker

This is a great resource for anticipating 70 of the most common social difficulties that students with autism may face. Handouts and activity ideas for each area provide the basis for instructing, modeling, and practicing these social skills with students.

(Shawnee Mission, KS: AAPC Publishing, 2003)

Super Skills: A Social Skills Group Program for Children With Asperger Syndrome, High-Functioning Autism, and Related Challenges, Judy Coucouvanis

This book provides everything needed to assess student needs, organize groups for instruction, and plan lessons in a comprehensive scope and sequence of critical social skills. The book is extremely user friendly and provides well-developed and simple-to-implement lesson plans and activities for a variety of age and skill levels.

(Shawnee Mission, KS: AAPC Publishing, 2005)

Resources for Behavior Intervention and Support

Asperger Syndrome and Difficult Moments: Practical Solutions for Tantrums, Rage, and Meltdowns (Revised and Expanded Edition), Brenda Smith Myles and Jack Southwick

This classic text offers both parents and professionals tried-and-true solutions to minimize the often frightening circumstances that surround the rage cycle – not only for the child with ASD but others in the environment as well. With a major section on interventions, this highly practical resource also focuses on the reactions of the adults around the child. The book takes the reader through the stages of the rage cycle and emphasizes the importance of utilizing the teachable moments before and after a rage episode.

(Shawnee Mission, KS: AAPC Publishing, 1995)

No More Meltdowns: Positive Strategies for Managing and Preventing Out-of-Control Behavior, Jed Baker

This book provides a solid foundation for understanding the most common triggers for emotional meltdowns as well as a framework for preventing them and then managing them when they do occur. The unique aspect of this book is its empowering emphasis on the parent or teacher examining and modifying his or her own reactions in the meltdown situation rather than focusing only on what the student needs to do differently.

(Arlington, TX: Future Horizons, 2008)

Resources for Sensory and Motor Support

Sensory Issues and High-Functioning Autism Spectrum and Related Disorders Practical Solutions for Making Sense of the World (2ⁿᵈ ed.), Brenda Myles, Kelly Mahler, and Lisa Robbins, L.

This book focuses on how many children with high-functioning ASD relate to the world through their senses with special emphasis on sensory integration and how the sensory systems impact behavior. Assessment tools can assist children in pinpointing sensory characteristics. Intervention strategies and case studies are also outlined.

(Shawnee Mission, KS: AAPC Publishing, 2014)

Yoga for Children With Autism Spectrum Disorders: A Step-by-Step Guide for Parents and Caregivers, Dion E. Betts

This well-illustrated and step-by-step guidebook offers excellent descriptions of yoga positions in a variety of sequences for calming, reducing stress, strengthening, and supporting sensory regulation. The sequences are of various lengths and can be customized based on individual student characteristics.

(Betts, 2006)

Practical Solutions for Stabilizing Students With Classic Autism to Be Ready to Learn: Getting to Go!, Judy Endow

This resource takes the unique and proactive approach of looking at improving student learning and behavior by exploring how educators can better support student sensory regulation. The book is written from the unique perspective of an individual on the autism spectrum who brings both a personal and professional perspective to explaining how a student's state of sensory regulation impacts his or her participation and learning in school.

(Shawnee Mission, KS: AAPC Publishing, 2011)

My Sensory Book: Working Together to Explore Sensory Issues and the Big Feelings They Cause: A Workbook for Parents, Professionals, and Children, Lauren H. Kerstein

This interactive learning tool helps students explore and understand their own sensory characteristics and empowers them to plan and use strategies that promote sensory modulation. The information is well organized into the different sensory systems and is presented in a way that is comprehensive enough to give educators a solid foundation of information but simple enough for students to understand and apply.

(Shawnee Mission, KS: AAPC Publishing, 2008)

A Buffet of Sensory Interventions: Solutions for Middle and High School Students With Autism Spectrum Disorders, Susan L. Culp

This tool provides a well-researched framework for helping adolescents better understand their sensory needs and plan options that can help them take control over their self-regulation. The well-organized format provides an enormous number of sensory strategies and makes a complex topic easy to navigate, understand, and apply to individual students.

(Shawnee Mission, KS: AAPC Publishing, 2011)

Resources for Classroom and Instructional Structure and Organization

The ASD NEST Model: A Framework for Inclusive Education for Higher Functioning Children With Autism Spectrum Disorders, Shirley Cohen and Lauren Houg (Eds.)

This well-researched and evidence-based program was formulated in response to the severe shortage of educational programs designed for higher functioning school-age children with ASD, which often leads to inappropriate placements, frequent changes in placement, and a lack of supports ... all of which inevitably results in ensured poor educational experiences. The program uses a positive behavior support approach and incorporates strategies that address areas of difficulty common in children with ASD, specifically sensory functioning, social relatedness, self-regulation, managing anxiety, and selective cognitive problems. This program helps children function comfortably and successfully in mainstream settings in their schools and communities, whenever feasible, with decreased need for professional support.

(Shawnee Mission, KS: AAPC Publishing, 2013)

Setting up Classroom Spaces That Support Students With Autism Spectrum Disorder, Susan Kabot and Christine Reeve

This resource is a "must have" for any teacher who is interested in setting up a classroom environment that will be conducive to the inclusion of students with autism. Well organized and clearly explained, with clear and abundant photographs, the authors provide practical strategies for creating visual and physical boundaries, supporting transitions, and reducing visual clutter, for maximum comfort and functionality in the education of children who benefit from a high degree of structure, predictability, and visual support.

(Shawnee Mission, KS: AAPC Publishing, 2010)

Building Independence: How to Create and Use Structured Work Systems, Christine Reeve and Susan Kabot

This is an excellent resource for understanding how to structure school work in a manner that maximizes students' success and promotes independence. Using simple, clear explanations accompanied by photographic examples, the authors show how to apply the foundational questions of structured work (What work is to be done? How much work is there? How do I know when I am done? What do I do next?) into tasks of various age and developmental levels. This resource is invaluable in helping teachers understand how best to structure work for students who need a high degree of consistency, predictability and structure.

(Shawnee Mission, KS: AAPC Publishing, 2012)

Resources for Individual Student Intervention Planning

The Ziggurat Model: A Framework for Designing Comprehensive Interventions for Individuals With High-Functioning Autism and Asperger Syndrome, Ruth Aspy and Barry Grossman

This resource is considered by many to be the "gold standard" for planning interventions for individuals on the autism spectrum. It provides a thorough understanding of the most common characteristics of individuals with autism, as well as evidence-based strategies for addressing them. The book includes checklists for assessing the characteristics of students as well as comprehensive planning forms to analyze the function of student behaviors and plan interventions to address the foundational needs of students on the autism spectrum.

(Shawnee Mission, KS: AAPC Publishing, 2008)

The Comprehensive Autism Planning System (CAPS) for Individuals With Autism Spectrum Disorders and Related Disabilities: Integrating Evidence-Based Practices Throughout the Student's Day (Second Edition), Shawn A. Henry and Brenda Smith Myles

This system allows educators to understand how to implement an instructional program for students with ASD. Known as CAPS, the model answers common questions about finding the right supports to fit a child's learning style in order to help him reach his full potential. Used with The Ziggurat Model (see above), CAPS enables educators and other professionals to address adequate yearly progress (AYP), response to intervention (RTI), and positive behavior support (PBS). This expanded second edition of CAPS adds important new material on technical assistance/consultation as well as up-to-date considerations of current mandates and trends that support CAPS use, including a major focus on evidence-based practices.

(Shawnee Mission, KS: AAPC Publishing, 2007)

Other AAPC Resources

Everyday Classroom Strategies and Practices for Supporting Children With Autism Spectrum Disorders

by Jamie D. Bleiweiss, PhD, Lauren Hough, MsEd, and Shirley Cohen, PhD

This practical approach to working with students with autism spectrum disorders helps to demystify the processes needed to help these students succeed and gives teachers the supports to plan appropriately for them. Adopted by several schools and districts, this timely resource clearly communicates how to create a classroom in which every learner succeeds with specific and easy-to-implement strategies for students who require minimal supports as well as those who require more intensive interventions. In compliance with current trends in education, it incorporates evidence-based practices, positive behavior supports, and uses Response to Intervention (RtI).

ISBN 9781937473815 Code 9105

Price: $34.95

Social Rules for Kids

The Top 100 Social Rules Kids Need to Succeed

by Sue Diamond, MA, CCC

Social Rules for Kids helps open the door of communication between parent and child by addressing 100 social rules for home, school and the community. Written directly to the student, these clear rules cover topics such as body language, manners and feelings. Reminders of appropriate social rules at the end of each page are combined into a complete list for easy reference.

ISBN 9781934575840 Code 9067

Price: $19.95

To order, please visit www.aapcpublishing.net

of Special Interest to General Educators

Simple Strategies That Work!

Helpful Hints for Educators of Students With Asperger Syndrome, High-Functioning Autism, and Related Disabilities

by Brenda Smith Myles, PhD, Diane Adreon, MA, and Dena Gitlitz

Another collaborative work from Brenda Smith Myles on proven simple strategies for the classroom. *Simple Strategies That Work!* provides teachers effective approaches and strategies to help students with ASD on the road to success. The book also discusses problems that may arise in the inclusion classroom and how educators can make even small adjustments to accommodate students with ASD, while not interfering with standard classroom routines.

ISBN 9781931282994
Code 9967

Price: $19.95

Starting Points

The Basics of Understanding and Supporting Children and Youth With Asperger Syndrome

by Jill Hudson and Brenda Smith Myles, PhD

Starting Points provides a global perspective on how the core characteristics of AS may appear separately or simultaneously, and how they may manifest in a variety of situations. Starting from the premise that no two individuals with Asperger Syndrome are the same, each characteristic is paired with a brief explanation, followed by a series of bulleted interventions that include strategies and visual supports to help children on the spectrum who have difficulty with abstract concepts and thoughts, difficulty understanding and regulating emotions, and difficulty recognizing, interpreting and empathizing with the emotions of others.

ISBN 9781934575086
Code 9995

Price: $17.95

Strategies at Hand

Quick and Handy Strategies for Working With Students on the Autism Spectrum

by Robin Brewer, EdD, and Tracy Mueller, PhD

This at-your-fingertips resource features easy-to-implement strategies that can be used in all types of educational settings and situations. The tool is broken down into five color-coded sections that are easy to locate and use: Learning Environments (classrooms and field trips), Areas of Student Need (communication and behavior), Transitions (substitute teachers and school assemblies), Alphabetical Explanations of Terms (functional behavioral assessment and picture communication systems) and Resources and References.

ISBN 9781934575185 |
Code 9004 | Price: $11.95

MORE ADVANCE REVIEWS ...

"Push to Open – A Teacher's QuickGuide to Universal Design for Teaching Students on the Autism Spectrum in the General Education Classroom is an invaluable resource that should be read and used by *all* educators. It communicates clearly how to create classrooms in which every learner can thrive, and provides readers with practical and user-friendly techniques and supports that can effectively enhance learning for all students. This book quite literally covers all the bases and offers a wealth of information that educators working with any student can use to ensure success in the classroom."
- Jamie D. Bleiweiss, PhD, assistant professor in special education, Hunter College, and author (with Hough and Cohen) of *Everyday Classroom Strategies and Practices for Supporting Children With Autism Spectrum Disorders*

"Lisa Combs has taken her expertise working with students on the autism spectrum and put it on paper! *Push to Open* is infused with current research but is still teacher friendly. This book will help educators in a variety of settings easily implement strategies for students across multiple disciplines and grade levels. I especially loved the QuickTip sheets at the end of the book, which is a culmination of strategies that are easy to implement. I highly recommend this book and I will be utilizing these strategies in my own classroom."
- Jennifer M. Schmidt, MEd, intervention specialist, Beavercreek High School; adjunct professor, Antioch McGregor Midwest

"Push to Open ... is a book that will open doors in classrooms and schools across the country. Educators are looking for tools to help them integrate their understanding of ASD into their teaching, and this tool will help them reach all learners by doing just that. The author supports the educator in the same way she expects the student to be supported in the classroom with thorough instruction and guided practice, consideration for differing modalities and perspectives, and with an expectation that each educator use the tools to open doors for students of all abilities. This is a book I'll share with my teachers, in book club format, helping them understand the ramifications of the choices we each make as we structure our classrooms."
- Katie White, MEd, principal, West Terrace Elementary School

"In this easy-to-read, practical guide, Combs provides the reader with a clear understanding of universal design for learning, the characteristics of the barriers that impede learning for students with ASD, as well as clearly defined strategies and methodologies that help remove those barriers while at the same time being effective for all learners. I highly recommend this book for any educator, administrator, service provider, and parent seeking to increase the participation and quality of learning engagement of students with ASD."
- Lisa Preston, special education supervisor

PUBLISHING

P.O. Box 23173
Shawnee Mission, Kansas 66283-0173
www.aapcpublishing.net

CPSIA information can be obtained
at www.ICGtesting.com
Printed in the USA
LVOW13s1253120517
534306LV00017B/405/P